ROYAL
SHAKESPEARE
COMPANY

THE ROMAN ACTOR
PHILIP MASSINGER

THIS EDITION PREPARED FOR THE
ROYAL SHAKESPEARE COMPANY

NICK HERN BOOKS
LONDON
www.nickhernbooks.co.uk

OTHER TITLES IN THIS SERIES

William Shakespeare
EDWARD III

Jonson, Marston and Chapman
EASTWARD HO!

John Fletcher
THE ISLAND PRINCESS

John Marston
THE MALCONTENT

––––––––––––––––––––

This edition of *The Roman Actor*
first published in Great Britain in 2002
as a paperback original by
Nick Hern Books Limited
14 Larden Road, London W3 7ST
in association with the
Royal Shakespeare Company

Cover design by RSC Graphics Department
Typeset by Country Setting, Kingsdown, Kent CT14 8ES
Printed by Biddles of Guildford

A CIP catalogue record for this book is available from
the British Library

ISBN 1 85459 697 7

THE ROYAL SHAKESPEARE COMPANY

The Royal Shakespeare Company is one of the world's best-known theatre ensembles.

The Company is widely regarded as one of the most important interpreters of Shakespeare and other dramatists. Today the RSC is at the leading edge of classical theatre, with an international reputation for artistic excellence, accessibility and high quality live performance.

Our mission at the Royal Shakespeare Company is to create outstanding theatre relevant to our times through the work of Shakespeare, other Renaissance dramatists, international and contemporary writers. Every year the Company plays to a million theatregoers at 2,000 performances, including over 50 weeks of UK and international touring.

We want to give as many people as possible, from all walks of life, a richer and fuller understanding and enjoyment of language and theatre. Through education and outreach programmes we continually strive to engage people with the experience of live performance.

The RSC's touchstone is the work of William Shakespeare. We are committed to presenting the widest range of Shakespeare's plays and demonstrating through performance the international and enduring appeal of his plays. We also want to inspire contemporary writers with the ambition of the Renaissance stage, presenting new plays alongside classical theatre.

The Company's roots in Stratford-upon-Avon stretch back to the nineteenth century. However, since the 1960s the RSC's work in Stratford has been complemented by a regular presence in London. But Stratford and London are only part of the story. Over 25 years of residency in the city of Newcastle upon Tyne have forged a profound link between RSC artists and audiences in the north east of England. Many of our productions also visit major regional theatres around Britain. And our annual regional tour sets up its own travelling auditorium in community centres, sport halls and schools in towns throughout the UK without access to professional theatre.

While the UK is the home of the Company, our audiences are global. The company regularly plays to enthusiastic theatregoers in other parts of Europe, across the United States, the Americas, Asia and Australasia. The RSC is proud of its relationships with partnering organisations in other countries, particularly in America.

Despite continual change, the RSC today is still at heart an ensemble Company. The continuation of this great tradition informs the work of all members of the Company. Directors, actors, dramatists and theatre practitioners all collaborate in the creation of the RSC's distinctive and unmistakable approach to theatre.

THE ROYAL SHAKESPEARE COMPANY

Patron Her Majesty The Queen
President His Royal Highness The Prince of Wales
Deputy President Sir Geoffrey Cass MA CIMgt
Chairman of the Board Lord Alexander of Weedon QC
Deputy Chairman Lady Sainsbury of Turville
Vice-Chairmen Charles Flower,
Professor Stanley Wells PhD, DIitt

DIRECTION
Artistic Director Adrian Noble
Managing Director Chris Foy
Executive Producer Lynda Farran
Advisory Direction John Barton, David Brierley,
Peter Brook, Trevor Nunn
Emeritus Directors Trevor Nunn, Terry Hands

ASSOCIATE DIRECTORS
Michael Attenborough *Principal Associate Director*
Michael Boyd, Gregory Doran, Steven Pimlott

CASTING
John Cannon CDG *Resident Casting Director*

COMPANY MANAGEMENT
Charles Evans *Company Manager (London)*

DEVELOPMENT
Liam Fisher-Jones *Development Director*
Paula Flinders *Head of Development*

DRAMATURGY
Paul Sirett *Dramaturg*
Zinnie Harris *Resident Playwright*

EDUCATION
Clare Venables *Director of Education*

FINANCE AND ADMINISTRATION
David Fletcher *Director of Finance and Administration*
Donna Gribben *Head of Finance*
Chris O'Brien *Head of Information Technology*
Elaine Smith *Senior Management Accountant*

HUMAN RESOURCES
Rachael Whitteridge *Head of Human Resources*
Gail Miller *Health and Safety Adviser*

MARKETING
Kate Horton *Director of Marketing*
Melanie Bloxham *Marketing Manager (Research and Development)*
Kathy Elgin *Head of Publications*
Chris Hill *Marketing Manager (Campaign)*
John Pinchbeck *Sales Manager*
Justin Tose *Retail Manager*
Andy Williams *Head of Graphics*

MUSIC
Stephen Warbeck *Head of Music & Associate Artist*
Kate Andrew *Music Manager*
Richard Brown *Director of Music (London)*
Tony Stenson *Music Director (London)*
Michael Tubbs *Music Advisor*
John Woolf *Company Music Director*

PLANNING ADMINISTRATION
Carol Malcolmson *Planning Administrator*

PRESS AND PUBLIC AFFAIRS
Roger Mortlock *Director of Press and Public Affairs*
Philippa Harland *Head of Press*
Peter Coombs *Community Liaison Officer*

PRODUCERS
Denise Wood *Producerr*

TECHNICAL AND PRODUCTION
Geoff Locker *Technical Director*
Simon Ash *Production Manager*
Alan Bartlett *Head of Construction*
Charlotte Bird *Head of Costume*
Simon Bowler *Head of Engineering Services*
Jeremy Dunn *Stratford Sound Manager*
John Evans *Property Workshop Manager*
Peter Fordham CEng *Engineering Manager (Stratford)*
Stuart Gibbons *Production Manager*
Jasper Gilbert *Production Manager*
Mark Graham *Production Manager*
Peter Griffin *Production Manager*
Michael Gunning *Lighting Supervisor*
Paul Hadland *Scenic Workshop Manager*
Roger Haymes *Stage Supervisor*
Vince Herbert *Head of Lighting*
Brenda Leedham *Head of Wigs and Make-up*
Nigel Loomes *Head of Paint Shop*
David Ludlam CEng *Engineering Manager (London)*
David Parker *Production Manager*
Anthony Rowe *Design Co-ordinator*
Barbara Stone *Maintenance Wardrobe*

PROJECTS
Caro MacKay *Project Administrator*
Martyn Sergent *Project Administrator*

STRATFORD REDEVELOPMENT
Jonathan Pope *Project Director*

THEATRE OPERATIONS
Neil Constable *London Manager*
Richard Rhodes *Theatres Manager (Stratford)*
Gary Stewart *Stratford Manager*

VOICE
Andrew Wade *Head of Voice*
Lyn Darnley *Senior Voice Coach*

The Royal Shakespeare Company is incorporated under Royal Charter.
Registered Charity Number 212481

A PARTNERSHIP WITH THE RSC

The RSC is immensely grateful for the valuable support of its corporate sponsors and individual and charitable donors. Between them these groups provide up to £6m a year for the RSC and support a range of initiatives such as actor training, education workshops and access to our performances for all members of society.

The RSC is renowned throughout the world as one of the finest arts brands. A corporate partnership offers unique and creative opportunities, both nationally and internationally, and benefits from our long and distinguished record of maintaining and developing relationships. Reaching over one million theatregoers a year, our Corporate Partnership programme progresses from Corporate Membership to Business Partnership to Season Sponsor to Title Sponsor, and offers the following benefits: extensive crediting and association; prestigious corporate hospitality; marketing and promotional initiatives; corporate citizenship and business networking opportunities. Our commitment to education, new writing and access provides a diverse portfolio of projects which offer new and exciting ways to develop partnerships which are non-traditional and mutually beneficial.

As an individual you may wish to support the work of the RSC through membership of the RSC Patrons. For as little as £21 per month you can join a cast drawn from our audience and the worlds of theatre, film, politics and business. Alternatively, the gift of a legacy to the RSC would enable the company to maintain and increase new artistic and educational work with children and adults through the Acting and Education Funds.

For information about corporate partnership with the RSC, please contact Victoria Okotie, Head of Corporate Partnerships,
Barbican Theatre, London EC2Y 8BQ.
Tel: **020 7382 7132**.
e-mail: **victoria.okotie@rsc.org.uk**

For information about individual relationships with the RSC, please contact Graeme Williamson, Development Manager,
Royal Shakespeare Theatre, Waterside,
Stratford-upon-Avon CV37 6BB.
Tel: **01789 412661**.
e-mail: **graemew@rsc.org.uk**

For information about RSC Patrons, please contact Julia Read, Individual Giving Manager,
Royal Shakespeare Theatre, Waterside, Stratford-upon-Avon CV37 6BB.
Tel: **01789 412661**.
e-mail: **julia.read@rsc.org.uk**

You can visit our web site at
www.rsc.org.uk/development

RSC EDUCATION

The objective of the RSC Education Department is to enable as many people as possible, from all walks of life, to have easy access to the great works of Shakespeare, the Renaissance and the theatre.

To do this, we are building a team which supports the productions that the Company presents onstage for the general public, special interest groups and for education establishments of all kinds.

We are also planning to develop our contribution as a significant learning resource in the fields of Shakespeare, the Renaissance, classical and modern theatre, theatre arts and the RSC. This resource is made available in many different ways, including workshops, teachers' programmes, summer courses, a menu of activities offered to group members of the audience, pre- and post-show events as part of the Events programme, open days, tours of the theatre, community activities and youth programmes. The RSC Collections, moved into a new home, will be used to create new programmes of learning and an expanded exhibition schedule.

We are developing the educational component of our new web site to be launched this year. The RSC will make use of appropriate new technologies to disseminate its work in many different ways to its many audiences.

We can also use our knowledge of theatre techniques to help in other aspects of learning: classroom teaching techniques for subjects other than drama or English, including management and personnel issues.

Not all of these programmes are available all the time, and not all of them are yet in place. However, if you are interested in pursuing any of these options, the telephone numbers and e-mail addresses are as follows:

For information on general education activities contact the Education Administrator, Sarah Keevill, on **01789 403462**, or e-mail her on **sarah.keevill @rsc.org.uk.**

To find out about backstage tours, please contact our Tour Manager, Anne Tippett on **01789 403405**, or e-mail her on **theatre.tours@rsc.org.uk.**

STAY IN TOUCH

For up-to-date news on the RSC, our productions and education work visit the RSC's official web site: **www.rsc.org.uk**. Information on RSC performances is also available on Teletext

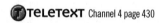 Channel 4 page 430

RSC MEMBERSHIP

Become an RSC Member and receive advance information and priority booking plus other exclusive benefits. Call our membership team on **01789 403440** for details of the various packages available, including UK membership, overseas, groups and education memberships. A free mailing list for those working in education is also available.

This production of *The Roman Actor* was first performed by the Royal Shakespeare Company
in the Swan Theatre, Stratford-upon-Avon, on 22 May 2002.
The original cast was as follows:

David Acton	Philargus
Paul Bhattacharjee	Ascletario
Antony Byrne	Parthenius
Billy Carter	Second Tribune
Wayne Cater	Aesopus
Shelley Conn	Julia
Joe Dixon	Paris
Amanda Drew	Domitilla
Geoffrey Freshwater	Sura
Jamie Glover	First Tribune
Sean Hannaway	Stephanos
Sian Howard	Caenis
Anna Madeley	Domitia
Michael Matus	Latinus
Keith Osborn	Lamia
Joshua Richards	Junius Rusticus
Antony Sher	Domitianus Caesar
Michael Thomas	Aretinus

Directed by	**Sean Holmes**
Designed by	**Antony Lamble**
Lighting designed by	**Wayne Dowdeswell**
Music by	**Adrian Lee**
Movement by	**Michael Ashcroft**
Fights by	**Terry King**
Sound designed by	**Martin Slavin**
Music Director	**Adrian Lee**
Casting Director	**Carrie Hilton**
Associate Director	**Heather Davies**
Production Managers	**Stuart Gibbons and Mark Graham**
Costume Supervisor	**Janet Bench**
Dialect Coach	**Jeannette Nelson**
Company voice work by	**Andrew Wade and Jeannette Nelson**
Company Manager	**Jondon**

Stage Manager	**Amanda McCaffrey**
Deputy Stage Manager	**Klare Roger**
Assistant Stage Manager	**Zoë Donegan**

This production was sponsored in Stratford-upon-Avon by

BIRMINGHAM
INTERNATIONAL AIRPORT

Plays for a Money-Get, Mechanic Age

In his *An Expostulation with Inigo Jones,* Ben Jonson quarrels with Jones about the growing supremacy of scenery and stage effects over the spoken text, in the masques they produced together at court.

> Pack with your peddling poetry to the stage,
> This is a money-get, mechanic age.

The stage, unlike the court where the masques were held, was a place to go and use your eyes and your ears, a place where language had primacy, where you went to hear a play.

The stages of the Rose and the Globe needed no scenery, that would be conjured by words, words spoken by the actor standing in the centre of a circle of ears. The Swan Theatre in Stratford reproduces just such a relationship between actor and audience: vital, immediate and dangerous.

Since the Swan opened in 1986, we have done many plays from Shakespeare's time, all Jonson's major comedies (though none of his tragedies), all the major pays of Marlowe and Webster, as well as plays by Middleton and Ford, Kyd, Tourneur, Heywood and even Shirley and Broome. This season, I have chosen plays with which audiences are likely to be less familiar and which reflect something of the range of the drama of the period, from City Comedy to Revenge Tragedy and much in between.

I've included *Edward III,* recently canonized from the Shakespeare Apocrypha; *The Malcontent* by the unjustly neglected John Marston (this is his RSC debut); Massinger's magnificent *The Roman Actor* (Adrian Noble directed the only other Massinger play we've done, *A New Way to Pay Old Debts* at The Other Place in 1983); *Eastward Ho!,* a collaboration by Jonson, Marston and George Chapman; and finally, representing the popular genre of travel plays, a discovery, *The Island Princess* set in the Spice Islands and written by John Fletcher (who collaborated with Shakespeare on *Henry VIII or All Is True,* which I directed in the Swan in 1996).

This season is unusual not just because of the concentration on these lesser known plays from the repertoire, but because this is the first time we have explored these works with a dedicated ensemble company of 28 actors, who will perform all five plays in close repertoire. The Swan Theatre allows us to achieve this turnover very swiftly.

Though we have often had very large and elaborate scenery in the Swan, it works perfectly well without any; allowing all the flexibility and fluidity of Shakespeare's theatre. Basically very little set is needed for any of these plays and without much scenery of course we can achieve a much faster turnaround of plays and spend more time rehearsing in the space where we'll perform. So we have decided to work faster than usual in order to achieve a full repertoire by midsummer. And who knows, perhaps other things will be released by working all together at this pace, a different dynamic, a closer collaborative spirit? These days we are used to discussing character and motivation at length in rehearsal. Neither of these words would have been understood by an actor in Shakespeare's day. The text was the character. And as far as we can tell there was very little rehearsal at all. Nowadays we are used to letting things cook more slowly in rehearsal, so let's see what more of a stir-fry mentality can achieve!

It's a punishing schedule, but our workloads look light in comparison with the actors in Shakespeare's day. In the 1594-5 season at the Rose Theatre, according to Philip Henslowe's Diary, the Lord Admiral's Men performed 38 plays, 21 of which were new! It's a fascinating statistic and one which reflects the audience's appetite for drama in that 'money-get mechanic age'. Jonson's phrase could well describe our own time, and perhaps begins to suggest why the plays of Shakespeare and his contemporaries echo and resonate so profoundly with our own.

GREGORY DORAN

March 2002

INTRODUCTION

The Roman Actor was written in 1626 for the King's Men, the company with which Shakespeare had been associated and which ran London's two leading playhouses, the Globe in Southwark and the fashionable Blackfriars theatre within the city walls. Its author, Philip Massinger, had just taken over as the King's Men's chief playwright on the death of John Fletcher, who performed this function in the years after Shakespeare's retirement.

Born in 1583, Massinger worked intermittently with the King's Men from 1616 onwards; during his twenty-five year career he gave them three dozen plays, some collaborative, the others unaided productions. *The Roman Actor* was the first play he wrote in his capacity as their house dramatist, and perhaps he chose its theatrical theme for the opportunity it presented of reflecting on his new position. Certainly he was proud of it, for when it was printed in 1629 he called it 'the most perfect birth of my Minerva'.

Although today Massinger is most remembered for his two great comedies, *A New Way to Pay Old Debts* (1625) and *The City Madam* (1632), his true bent lay in tragicomedy and tragedy. The satire of the comedies is very dark: their villains are outrageous egotists and power-seekers whose ambitions are reined in only when ruthless violence is used against them. Such violence makes Massinger's comedy unsettling, and suggests how ill-sorted with humour was his view of the world. A sombre and reflective writer whose plays contain not one line of prose, Massinger liked to depict societies that are riven with non-negotiable differences, and to put his characters in dilemmas that are radically contradictory and generate sustained ethical debate, usually with lurking political implications. He often leaves his final scenes painfully unresolved, with loose ends that suggest little has really been concluded.

The signature theme to which Massinger repeatedly returned was the tension between individual freedom and collective rule, the recurrent collision between the liberty of the weak and the control of the strong – whether in the corridors of power as subjects struggle with over-mighty princes, or as conflicts over personal autonomy in the smaller spaces of home. A distant connection of the Earl of Pembroke, to whom his father was steward, Massinger was wedded to the idea that society ought to be an integrated fabric in which caring patriarchs ruled justly and responsibly over their subjects or families. As the page Alworth says to his lord in *A New Way to Pay Old Debts*, 'You have been more like a father to me than a master'. However, Massinger's idealism was toughened by low expectations that this social contract would be fulfilled, or that rationality would generally prevail.

In *The Roman Actor*, both responsibility and reason are thin on the ground. *The Roman Actor* is one of several early seventeenth-century plays that focus on the history of Rome under the Caesars. The best-known is Ben Jonson's tragedy *Sejanus* (1603), which depicts the devious relationships between the emperor Tiberius, his henchmen and opponents. Others include an anonymous *Tragedy of Nero* (1624?); Thomas May's *Julia Agrippina* (1628), which deals with the death of Claudius and the rise of Nero; and Nathaniel Richards's *Messallina* (1635?), on the promiscuous love-life of Claudius's empress. All these plays hark back to the Roman historian Tacitus, and they inherit Tacitus's anxiety about the workings of empire. They represent the imperial court as a place of vice and corruption, and focus on the arts of power, the stratagems by which the emperors achieve their stranglehold over the state. At a time when Machiavelli was unavailable in English, Tacitus showed how rule could be maintained by expediency, pragmatism and sheer force of will. Readers absorbed his lessons with a mix of fear and fascination.

It is tempting to see this obsession with Rome as a response to contemporary uncertainties. All across Europe, princely dynasties were enlarging their power, while parliaments and assemblies were falling into abeyance – a process well under way in early Stuart England, where, to the concern of many, parliament was often absent for long periods. The Stuart monarchs were especially keen on layering their imagery of kingship with imperial resonances. At his coronation, James I was hailed as a new Augustus, bringing peace to his nation and renewing lost empires, while in his court entertainments Charles I liked to dance in the role of triumphant emperor, achieving symbolic victories in stupendous classical cityscapes. Massinger's fourth scene shows Caesar entering Rome in triumph, possibly an echo of Charles's (actually low-key) coronation earlier that same year. In 1628, Charles would consolidate his Roman iconography by buying Mantegna's *Triumphs of Caesar* – eight huge canvases still hanging today at Hampton Court – for a stupendous sum from the Duke of Mantua.

Massinger alludes to current political dilemmas most clearly in the episode in which Caesar relieves the senator Lamia of his wife. For Lamia, this is a shocking violation of law and ownership:

> Cannot a man be master of his wife
> Because she's young and fair, without a patent?
> I in mine own house am an emperor,
> And will defend what's mine.

But Lamia's belief in the sanctity of property is easily overridden by imperial command – 'When power puts in its plea, the laws are silenced', says Caesar's servant Parthenius – and by his wife's disconcerting willingness to follow the money. If she is going to be possessed, evidently she would prefer that the emperor be her owner. In the events that follow, Domitian's disregard for the law is played out as a pursuit of sensual excess. Driven by lust and cruelty, he displays his power by having his will in contempt of all who stand in its way, and indulging his pleasures to the hilt, no matter how deleterious their consequences for his subjects. This self-indulgence is both morally and politically dangerous, since his abdication to desire instates a principle of anarchy at the heart of empire. He is unfit to rule Rome because he is unable to rule himself.

However, this political analysis is complicated by Massinger's focus on the Roman actor, Paris, and by his sense of theatre's ambiguous involvement in the anarchy that it critiques. The story begins with a debate over the value of drama, in which Paris responds to charges of sedition and libel with the defence that theatre is essentially ethical. Its plots do not attack individuals, and it upholds morality by showing virtue rewarded and vice punished. His oration has been much admired, and was popular in the nineteenth century as an independent stage-piece in its own right. But in context its impact is different, since once Paris is commanded to perform at court, his high-minded ideas start to unravel. The first play, intended as a satire on greed, fails to persuade its viewers; the second has unfortunate effects, as his acting strikes Domitian's mistress in love with him; and the third ends violently, with the real death of the actor. Massinger alludes to the supposed historical fact that some Roman emperors performed in tragedies opposite condemned criminals, forcing them to play characters destined to die, so that they received their deaths in earnest from the emperor's own hand. But this device allows him to put a question mark over the drama's immunity to the excess that characterizes Domitian's Rome. Far from being a moral laboratory, theatre too is marked by violence and desire.

It seems unlikely that Massinger meant to undermine his own profession. Still, Paris's experiences do concede some of the points that puritans levelled against the contemporary stage: that plays need to represent vice in order to censure it, that they blend fiction with reality, and make unpredictable emotional demands on their spectators. Theatre's aesthetic effect is both the source of its power and what makes it potentially disturbing to the state. Moreover, Paris's dilemma resembles that of the early Stuart playing companies: his profession is awkwardly poised between commercial subordination to a fickle public and an equally problematic sponsorship by the court. In the first scene, the actors complain that takings are falling off, but although Domitian's patronage is more rewarding, it draws Paris into a world where he has even less control over his life and craft. Considering the prestige and protection of imperial patronage, it is unsurprising that Paris welcomes it, but the costs of his dependence prove to be disastrous.

At the end, Massinger will leave these contradictions hanging. Given his professional affiliations, there was no way that Paris could avoid the catastrophe that overtakes him. As for Domitian, he gets his come-uppance, but it is difficult to feel that the avengers are endorsed. A loose coalition who unite out of essentially private grievances, they lack a common ideology, and the tribunes who arrest them seem unlikely to forgive a murder, no matter how monstrous the tyrant was. The only entirely moral position belongs to the stoical senators, Rusticus and Sura, who, in the third act, endure with 'passive fortitude' the tortures with which Caesar tries to vex them. The 'spectacle' of their patience under torment enrages Domitian and reduces the other on-lookers to helpless horror. It is perhaps the ultimate and most alarming display of extreme theatre in this play that reflects so profoundly on its own art.

MARTIN BUTLER
University of Leeds

NTax.

THE ROMAN ACTOR

CHARACTERS

Domitianus Caesar
Paris, *the tragedian*
Parthenius, *a freeman of Caesar's*
Aelius Lamia
Stephanos
Junius Rusticus
Aretinus Clemens
Aesopus, *a player*
Philargus, *a rich miser*
Palphurius Sura, *a senator*
Fulcinius, *a senator*
Latinus, *a player*
Ascletario, *an astrologer*
Sejeius and Entellus, *conspirators*
Tribunes
Lictors
Domitia, *the wife of Aelius Lamia*
Domitilla, *cousin-german to Caesar*
Julia, *Titus's daughter*
Caenis, *Vespasian's concubine*

A centurion, captains, soldiers, guards servants, a lady

Enter Paris, Latinus and Aesopus

Aesopus	What do we act today?
Latinus	Agave's frenzy,

With Pentheus' bloody end.

Paris   It skills not what;
The times are dull, and all that we receive
Will hardly satisfy the day's expense.
Those that reign in every noble family
Declaim against us; and our amphitheatre,
Great Pompey's work, that hath giv'n full delight
Both to the eye and ear of fifty thousand
Spectators in one day, as if it were
Some unknown desert, or great Rome unpeopl'd,
Is quite forsaken.

Latinus   Pleasures of worse natures
Are gladly entertain'd, and they that shun us
Practise, in private, sports the stews would blush at.
A litter borne by eight Liburnian slaves,
To buy diseases from a glorious strumpet,
The most censorious of our Roman gentry,
Nay, of the guarded robe, the senators,
Esteem an easy purchase.

Paris   Yet grudge us
(That with delight join profit, and endeavour
To build their minds up fair, and on the stage
Decipher to the life what honours wait

On good and glorious actions, <u>and the shame</u>
<u>That treads upon the heels of vice</u>) the salary
Of six sestertii.

Aesopus   For the profit, Paris,
And mercenary gain, they are things beneath us,
Since while you hold your grace and power with Caesar,
We from your bounty find a large supply,
Nor can one thought of want ever approach us.

Paris   Our aim is glory, and to leave our names
To aftertimes.

Latinus   And would they give us leave,
There ends all our ambition.

Aesopus   We have enemies,
And great ones too, I fear. 'Tis given out lately
The consul Aretinus, Caesar's spy,
Said at his table, ere a month expir'd,
For being gall'd in our last comedy,
He would silence us for ever.

Paris   I expect
No favour from him; my strong Aventine is
That great Domitian, whom we oft have cheer'd
In his most sullen moods, will once return,
Who can repair with ease the consul's ruins.

Latinus   'Tis frequent in the city, he hath subdu'd
The Catti and the Daci, and ere long,
The second time will enter Rome in triumph.

            Enter two Lictors ROMAN OFFICIAL, aided Magistrates IN MaKING aRRESTS.

Paris   Jove hasten it! – With us? – I now believe
The consul's threats, Aesopus.

First Lictor   You are summon'd
T'appear today in Senate.

Second Lictor	And there to answer
	What shall be urg'd against you.
Paris	We obey you.
	Nay, droop not, fellows; innocence should be bold.
	We that have personated in the scene
	The ancient heroes and the falls of princes
	With loud applause, being to act ourselves,
	Must do it with undaunted confidence.
	Whate'er our sentence be, think 'tis in sport;
	And though condemn'd, let's hear it without sorrow,
	As if we were to live again tomorrow.
First Lictor	'Tis spoken like yourself.

Enter Aelius Lamia, Junius Rusticus, Palphurius Sura

Lamia	Whither goes Paris?
First Lictor	He's cited to the Senate.
Latinus	I am glad the state is
	So free from matters of more weight and trouble
	That it has vacant time to look on us.
Paris	That reverend place, in which the affairs of kings
	And provinces were determin'd, to descend
	To the censure of a bitter word, or jest,
	Dropp'd from a poet's pen! Peace to your lordships!
	We are glad that you are safe.

Exeunt Lictors, Paris, Latinus, Aesopus

Lamia	What times are these?
	To what is Rome fall'n? May we, being alone,
	Speak our thoughts freely of the prince and state,
	And not fear the informer?
Rusticus	Noble Lamia,
	So dangerous the age is, and such bad acts
	Are practis'd everywhere, we hardly sleep,

King Lear

Nay, cannot dream, with safety. All our actions
Are call'd in question; sons accuse their fathers,
Fathers their sons; and but to win a smile
From one in grace at court, our chastest matrons
Make shipwreck of their honours. To be virtuous
Is to be guilty. They are only safe
That know to soothe the prince's appetite,
And serve his lusts.

Sura
'Tis true; and 'tis my wonder
That two sons of so different a nature
Should spring from good Vespasian. We had a Titus,
Who did esteem that day lost in his life
In which some one or other tasted not
Of his magnificent bounties. One that had
A ready tear when he was forc'd to sign
The death of an offender.

Lamia
Yet his brother
Domitian, that now sways the power of things,
Is so inclin'd to blood that no day passes
In which some are not fasten'd to the hook,
Or thrown down from the Gemonies. His freemen
Scorn the nobility, and he himself,
As if he were not made of flesh and blood,
Forgets he is a man.

Rusticus
In his young years
He show'd what he would be when grown to ripeness:
His greatest pleasure was, being a child,
With a sharp-pointed bodkin to kill flies,
Whose rooms now men supply. For his escape
In the Vitellian war, he rais'd a temple
To Jupiter, and proudly plac'd his figure
In the bosom of the god. And in his edicts
He does not blush, or start, to style himself
(As if the name of emperor were base)
Great Lord and God Domitian.

Sura   I have letters
He's on his way to Rome, and purposes
To enter with all glory. The flattering Senate
Decrees him divine honours, and to cross it
Were death with studied torments. For my part,
I will obey the time; it is in vain
To strive against the torrent.

Rusticus   Let's to the Curia,
And though unwillingly, give our suffrages
Before we are compell'd.

Lamia   And since we cannot
With safety use the active, let's make use of
The passive fortitude, with this assurance
That the state, sick in him, the gods to friend,
Though at the worst will now begin to mend.

                                        Exeunt

SCENE TWO

Enter Domitia, and Parthenius with a letter.

Domitia   To me this reverence?

Parthenius   I pay it, lady,
Dominian's
Freeman   As a debt due to her that's Caesar's mistress,
For understand with joy, he that commands
All that the sun gives warmth to, is your servant.
Be not amaz'd, but fit you to your fortunes.
Think upon state, and greatness, and the honours
That wait upon Augusta – for that name
Ere long comes to you. Still you doubt your vassal;
But when you've read this letter, writ and sign'd

With his imperial hand, you will be freed
From fear and jealousy, and I beseech you,
When all the beauties of the earth bow to you,
And senators shall take it for an honour,
As I do now, to kiss these happy feet,
Think on Parthenius.

Domitia   Rise! I am transported
And hardly dare believe what is assur'd here.
The means, my good Parthenius, that wrought Caesar
(Our god on earth) to cast an eye of favour
Upon his humble handmaid?

Parthenius   What but your beauty?
When nature fram'd you for her masterpiece,
As the pure abstract of all rare in woman,
She had no other ends but to design you
To the most eminent place. I will not say
(For it would smell of arrogance t'insinuate
The service I have done you) with what zeal
I oft have made relation of your virtues,
Or how I have sung your goodness.

Domitia   You are modest;
And were it in my power I would be thankful.
If that, when I was mistress of myself,
And in my way of youth, pure and untainted,
The emperor had vouchsaf'd to seek my favours,
I had with joy given up my virgin fort
At the first summons to his soft embraces;
But I am now another's, not mine own.
You know I have a husband. For my honour
I would not be his strumpet; and how law
Can be dispens'd with to become his wife,
To me's a riddle.

Parthenius   I can soon resolve it.
When power puts in its plea the laws are silenc'd;

The world confesses one Rome, and one Caesar,
And, as his rule is infinite, his pleasures
Are unconfin'd; this syllable, his will,
Stands for a thousand reasons.

Domitia   But with safety
(Suppose I should consent) how can I do it?
My husband is a senator of a temper
Not to be jested with.

Enter Lamia

Parthenius   As if he durst
Be Caesar's rival! Here he comes; with ease
I will remove this scruple.

Lamia   How! So private!
Mine own house made a brothel! Sir, how durst you,
Though guarded with your power in court, and
                                        greatness,
Hold conference with my wife? As for you, minion,
I shall hereafter treat –

Parthenius   You are rude and saucy,
Nor know to whom you speak.

Lamia   This is fine, i'faith!

Parthenius Your wife! But touch her, and think what 'tis to die.
Not to lose time, she's Caesar's choice.
It is sufficient honour
You were his taster in this heavenly nectar,
But now must quit the office.

Lamia   This is rare!
Cannot a man be master of his wife
Because she's young, and fair, without a patent?
I in mine own house am an emperor,
And will defend what's mine. Where are my knaves?
If such an insolence escape unpunish'd –

Parthenius	– In yourself, Lamia.

Stamps

Enter a Centurion with Soldiers

Lamia   The Guard! Why, am I
Design'd for death?

Domitia   As you desire my favour
Take not so rough a course.

Parthenius   All your desires
Are absolute commands. Yet give me leave
To put the will of Caesar into act.

words = things

Offers a paper

Here's a bill of divorce between your lordship
And this great lady. If you refuse to sign it,
And so as if you did it uncompell'd,
Won to it by reasons that concern yourself,
Her honour, too, untainted, here are clerks
Shall in your best blood write it new, till torture
Compel you to perform it.

Lamia   Is this legal?

Parthenius   Will you dispute?

Lamia   I know not what to urge
Against myself, but too much dotage on her,
Love and observance.

Parthenius   Set it under your hand
That you are impotent, and cannot pay
The duties of a husband, or that you are mad;
Rather than want just cause, we'll make you so.
Dispatch, you know the danger else. Deliver it.

Lamia writes

Nay, on your knee. – Madam, you now are free,
And mistress of yourself.

Lamia   Can you, Domitia,
Consent to this?

Domitia   'Twould argue a base mind
To live a servant, when I may command.
I now am Caesar's, and yet, in respect
I once was yours, when you come to the palace
(Provided you deserve it in your service)
You shall find me your good mistress. Wait me,
                                        Parthenius;
And now farewell, poor Lamia!

                                    Exeunt all but Lamia

Lamia   To the gods
I bend my knees (for tyranny hath banish'd
Justice from men), and humbly invoke 'em
That this my ravish'd wife may prove as fatal
To proud Domitian, and her embraces
Afford him in the end as little joy,
As wanton Helen brought to him of Troy.   *Exit*

SCENE THREE

*Enter Lictors, Aretinus, Fulcinius, Rusticus,
Sura, Paris, Latinus, Aesopus*

Lictors   Silence!

Aretinus   The purpose of this frequent Senate
Is first to give thanks to the gods of Rome
That for the propagation of the empire

Vouchsafe us one to govern it like themselves.
In height of courage, depth of understanding,
And all those virtues and remarkable graces
Which make a prince most eminent, our Domitian
Transcends the ancient Romans. I can never
Bring his praise to a period. For he has
Pompey's dignity, Augustus' state,
Antony's bounty, and great Julius' fortune,
With Cato's resolution. I am lost
In th'ocean of his virtues. In a word,
All excellencies of good men in him meet,
But no part of their vices.

Rusticus   This is no flattery!

Sura   Take heed, you'll be observ'd.

Aretinus   'Tis then most fit that we
Should not connive and see his government
Deprav'd and scandalis'd by meaner men
That to his favour and indulgence owe
Themselves and being.

Paris   Now he points at us.

Aretinus   Cite Paris, the tragedian.

Paris   Here.

Aretinus   Stand forth.
In thee, as being the chief of thy profession,
I do accuse the quality of treason,
As libellers against the state and Caesar.

Paris   Mere accusations are not proofs, my lord.
In what are we delinquents?

Aretinus   You are they
That search into the secrets of the time,
And under feign'd names on the stage present

Actions not to be touch'd at, and traduce
Persons of rank, and quality, of both sexes,
And with satirical and bitter jests
Make even the senators ridiculous
To the plebeians.

punished for mockery in theater

Paris   If I free not myself
(And in myself the rest of my profession)
From these false imputations, and prove
That they make that a libel which the poet
Writ for a comedy, so acted too,
It is but justice that we undergo
The heaviest censure.

Aretinus   Are you on the stage,
You talk so boldly?

Paris   The whole world being one,
This place is not exempted, and I am
So confident in the justice of our cause
That I could wish Caesar (in whose great name
All kings are comprehended) sat as judge,
To hear our plea, and then determine of us.
If to express a man sold to his lusts,
Wasting the treasure of his time and fortunes
In wanton dalliance, and to what sad end
A wretch that's so given over does arrive at,
Deterring careless youth, by his example,
From such licentious courses, laying open
The snares of bawds, and the consuming arts
Of prodigal strumpets, can deserve reproof,
Why are not all your golden principles,
Writ down by grave philosophers to instruct us
To choose fair virtue for our guide, not pleasure,
Condemn'd unto the fire?

audience

purpose

Sura   There's spirit in this.

Paris

Or if desire of honour was the base
On which the building of the Roman empire
Was rais'd up to this height; if to inflame
The noble youth with an ambitious heat
T'endure the frosts of danger may deserve
Reward or favour from the commonwealth
Actors may put in for as large a share
As all the sects of the philosophers.
They with cold precepts (perhaps seldom read)
Deliver what an honourable thing
The active virtue is. But does that fire
The blood, or swell the veins with emulation
To be both good and great, equal to that
Which is presented on our theatres?
Let a good actor in a lofty scene
Show great Alcides honour'd in the sweat
Of his twelve labours; or a bold Camillus
Forbidding Rome to be redeem'd with gold
From the insulting Gauls. If done to the life,
As if they saw their dangers and their glories,
And did partake with them in their rewards,
All that have any spark of Roman in them,
The slothful arts laid by, contend to be
Like those they see presented.

Rusticus

He has put
The consuls to their whisper.

Paris

But 'tis urg'd
That we corrupt youth, and traduce superiors.
When do we bring a vice upon the stage
That does go off unpunish'd? Do we teach,
By the success of wicked undertakings,
Others to tread in their forbidden steps?
Even those spectators that were so inclin'd
Go home chang'd men. And, for traducing such
That are above us, publishing to the world

Their secret crimes, we are as innocent
As such as are born dumb. When we present
An heir that does conspire against the life
Of his dear parent, if there be
Among the auditors one whose conscience tells him
He is of the same mould, we cannot help it.
Or bringing on the stage a loose adult'ress
That does maintain the riotous expense
Of him that feeds her greedy lust, yet suffers
To starve the while for hunger, if a matron,
However great in fortune, birth or titles,
Guilty of such a foul, unnatural sin,
Cry out, ''Tis writ by me', we cannot help it.
Or when we show a judge that is corrupt,
And will give up his sentence as he favours
The person, not the cause, saving the guilty,
If of his faction, and as oft condemning
The innocent out of particular spleen,
If any of this reverend assembly,
Nay, e'en yourself, my lord, that are the image
Of absent Caesar, feel something in your bosom
That puts you in remembrance of things past
Or things intended, 'tis not in us to help it.
I have said, my lord; and now, as you find cause,
Or censure us or free us with applause.

Latinus Well pleaded, on my life! I never saw him
Act an orator's part before.

                              A shout within

                    Enter Parthenius

Aretinus   What shout is that?

Parthenius Caesar, our lord, married to conquest, is
Return'd in triumph.

Fulcinius   Let's all haste to meet him.

Aretinus	Break up the court; we will reserve to him The censure of this cause.
All	Long life to Caesar!

Exeunt

SCENE FOUR

Enter Julia, Caenis, Domitilla, Domitia

Caenis	Stand back. The place is mine.
Julia	Yours? Am I not Great Titus' daughter, and Domitian's niece? Dares any claim precedence?
Caenis	I was more: The mistress of your father, and in his right Claim duty from you.
Julia	I confess you were useful To please his appetite.
Domitia	To end the controversy – For I'll have no contending – I'll be bold To lead the way myself.
Domitilla	You, minion!
Domitia	Yes; And all ere long shall kneel to catch my favours.
Julia	Whence springs this flood of greatness?
Domitia	You shall know Too soon, for your vexation, and perhaps Repent too late, and pine with envy when You see whom Caesar favours.

Julia	Observe the sequel.

*Enter at one door Captains with laurels, Domitian Caesar
in his triumphant chariot, Parthenius, Paris, Latinus, Aesopus;
met by Aretinus, Sura, Lamia, Rusticus, Fulcinius,
with Prisoners led by him*

Caesar	As we now touch the height of human glory,
	Riding in triumph to the Capitol,
	Let these, whom this victorious arm hath made
	The scorn of fortune and the slaves of Rome,
	Taste the extremes of misery. Bear them off
	To the common prisons, and there let them prove
	How sharp our axes are!

Exeunt Captains with Prisoners

Rusticus	A bloody entrance!
Caesar	To tell you you are happy in your prince
	Were to distrust your love or my desert,
	And either were distasteful. Or to boast
	How much, not by my deputies but myself,
	I have enlarg'd the empire; or what horrors
	The soldier in our conduct hath broke through,
	Would better suit the mouth of Plautus' braggart
	Than the adored monarch of the world.
Sura	This is no boast!
Caesar	When I but name the Daci
	And grey-ey'd Germans, whom I have subdu'd,
	The ghost of Julius will look pale with envy,
	And great Vespasian's and Titus' triumph
	Will be no more remember'd. I am above
	All honours you can give me; and the style
	Of Lord and God, which thankful subjects give me
	(Not my ambition), is deserv'd.
Aretinus	At all parts

Celestial sacrifice is fit for Caesar
In our acknowledgement.

Caesar   Thanks, Aretinus;
Still hold our favour. I cannot think
That there is one among you so ungrateful,
Or such an enemy to thriving virtue,
That can esteem the jewel he holds dearest
Too good for Caesar's use.

Sura   All we possess –

Lamia   Our liberties –

Fulcinius   Our children –

Parthenius   Wealth –

Aretinus   And throats
Fall willingly beneath his feet.

Rusticus   Base flattery!
What Roman could endure this?

Caesar   This calls on
My love to all, which spreads itself among you.
[*To the women*]
The beauties of the time! Receive the honour
To kiss the hand, which rear'd up thus, holds thunder.
To you 'tis an assurance of a calm.
Julia, my niece, and Caenis, the delight
Of old Vespasian; Domitilla, too,
A princess of our blood.

Rusticus   'Tis strange his pride
Affords no greater courtesy to ladies
Of such high birth and rank.

Sura   Your wife's forgotten.

Lamia   No, she will be remember'd, fear it not;
She will be grac'd, and greas'd.

Caesar	But when I look on
	Divine Domitia, methinks we should meet
	(The lesser gods applauding the encounter)
	As Jupiter embrac'd his Juno.
	Lamia, 'tis your honour that she's mine.
Lamia	You are too great to be gainsaid.
Caesar	Let all
	That fear our frown, or do affect our favour,
	Without examining the reason why,
	Salute her (by this kiss I make it good)
	With the title of Augusta.
Domitia	Still your servant.
All	Long live Augusta, great Domitian's empress!
Caesar	Paris, my hand.
Paris	The gods still honour Caesar.
Caesar	The wars are ended, and, our arms laid by,
	We are for soft delights. Command the poets
	To use their choicest and most rare invention
	To entertain the time, and be you careful
	To give it action. We'll provide the people
	Pleasures of all kinds. – My Domitia, think not
	I flatter, though thus fond. – On to the Capitol!
	'Tis death to him that wears a sullen brow.
	This 'tis to be a monarch, when alone
	He can command all, but is aw'd by none.

Exeunt

ACT TWO

SCENE ONE

Enter Philargus, Parthenius

Philargus	My son to tutor me! Know your obedience,
	And question not my will.
Parthenius	Sir, did the suit that I prefer to you
	Concern myself, and aim'd not at your good,
	You might deny, and I sit down with patience,
	And after never press you.
Philargus	I'the name of Pluto
	What wouldst thou have me do?
Parthenius	Right to yourself;
	Or suffer me to do it. Can you imagine
	This nasty hat, this tatter'd cloak, rent shoe,
	This sordid linen, can become the master
	Of your fair fortunes, whose superfluous means
	Could clothe you in the costliest Persian silks
	And every day fresh change of Tyrian purple?
Philargus	Out upon thee!
	My moneys in my coffers melt to hear thee.
	Shall I make my tailor or jeweller my heir?
	No, I hate pride.
Parthenius	Yet decency would do well.
	Though for your outside you will not be alter'd,
	Let me prevail so far yet, as to win you
	Not to deny your belly nourishment,
	Neither to think you have feasted when 'tis cramm'd
	With mouldy barley-bread, onions, and leeks,
	And the drink of bondmen, water.

Philargus	Wouldst thou have me

Go riot out my state in curious sauces?
Wise nature with a little is contented,
And following her, my guide, I cannot err.

Parthenius   But you destroy her in your want of care
(I blush to see and speak it) to maintain her
In perfect health and vigour, when you suffer
(Frighted with the charge of physic) rheums, catarrhs,
The scurf, ache in your bones, to grow upon you,
And hasten on your fate with too much sparing,
When a cheap purge, a vomit, and good diet
May lengthen it. Give me but leave to send
The emperor's doctor to you.

Philargus   I'll be borne first
Half-rotten to the fire that must consume me!
No, I'll not lessen my dear golden heap,
Which every hour increasing does renew
My youth and vigour. Let me enjoy it,
And brood o'er't, while I live; it being my life,
My soul, my all. But when I turn to dust,
Inherit thou my adoration of it,
And, like me, serve my idol.

Exit Philargus

Parthenius   What a strange torture
Is avarice to itself! Some course I must take,
To make my father know what cruelty
He uses on himself.

Enter Paris

Paris   Sir, with your pardon,
I make bold to inquire the emperor's pleasure;
For, being by him commanded to attend,
Your favour may instruct us what's his will
Shall be this night presented.

Parthenius   My lov'd Paris,
Without my intercession you well know
You may make your own approaches, since his ear
To you is ever open.

Paris   I acknowledge
His clemency to my weakness. And if ever
I do abuse it, lightning strike me dead!
The grace he pleases to confer upon me
(Without boast I may say so much) was never
Employ'd to wrong the innocent, or to incense
His fury.

Parthenius   'Tis confess'd many men owe you
For provinces they ne'er hoped for; and their lives,
Forfeited to his anger. You being absent,
I could say more.

Paris   You still are my good patron;
And lay it in my fortune to deserve it.

Parthenius   Met you my father?

Paris   Yes, sir, with much grief
To see him as he is. Can nothing work him
To be himself?

Parthenius   Oh, Paris, 'tis a weight
Sits heavy here, but he is deaf
To all persuasion.

Paris   Sir, with your pardon,
I'll offer my advice. I once observ'd
In a tragedy of ours, in which a murder
Was acted to the life, a guilty hearer
Forc'd by the terror of a wounded conscience
To make discovery of that which torture
Could not wring from him.
Now could you but persuade the emperor

To see a comedy we have that's styl'd
The Cure of Avarice, and to command
Your father to be a spectator of it,
I think that he, looking on a covetous man
Presented on the stage, as in a mirror,
May see his own deformity, and loathe it.

Parthenius   [*Gives him money*] There's your fee;
I ne'er bought better counsel. Be you in readiness,
I will effect the rest.

Paris   Sir, when you please,
We'll be prepar'd to enter. – Sir, the emperor.

                                        Exit Paris

              Enter Caesar, Aretinus, Guard

Caesar   Repine at us?

Aretinus   'Tis more, or my informers
That keep strict watch upon him are deceiv'd
In their intelligence.

                              Gives him a paper

                      There is a list
Of malcontents, as Junius Rusticus,
Palphurius Sura, and this Aelius Lamia,
That murmur at your triumphs as mere pageants,
And at their midnight meetings tax your justice
(For so I style what they call tyranny)
For the death of the philosopher Thrasea,
As if in him Virtue herself were murder'd.
Nor forget they your much love
To Julia your niece, censur'd as incest,
And done in scorn of Titus, your dead brother;
But the divorce Lamia was forc'd to sign
To her you honour with Augusta's title
Being only nam'd, they do conclude there was

A Lucrece once, a Collatine, and a Brutus;
But nothing Roman left now, but in you
The lust of Tarquin.

Caesar   Yes. His fire and scorn
Of such as think that our unlimited power
Can be confin'd. Dares Lamia pretend
An interest to that which I call mine?
Or but remember she was ever his,
That's not in our possession? Fetch him hither!

The Guard goes off

I'll give him cause to wish he rather had
Forgot his own name than e'er mention'd hers.
Shall we be circumscrib'd? Am I master
Of two and thirty legions, that awe
All nations of the triumphed world,
Yet tremble at our frown? Yield an account
Of what's our pleasure to a private man?
Rome perish first, and Atlas' shoulders shrink,
Heav'n's fabric fall; the sun, the moon, the stars
Losing their light, and comfortable heat,
Ere I confess that any fault of mine
May be disputed!

Aretinus   So you preserve your power
As you should: equal, and omnipotent here,
With Jupiter's above.

Parthenius kneeling, whispers to Caesar

Caesar   Thy suit is granted,
Whate'er it be, Parthenius, for thy service
Done to Augusta. Only so? A trifle.
Command him hither. If the comedy fail
To cure him, I will minister something to him
That shall instruct him to forget his gold,
And think upon himself.

Parthenius	May it succeed well,
	Since my intents are pious.

Exit Parthenius

Caesar   We are resolv'd
What course to take, and therefore, Aretinus,
Inquire no farther. Go you to my empress,
And say I do entreat (for she rules him
Whom all men else obey) she would vouchsafe
The music of her voice at yonder window,
When I advance my hand thus.

Exit Aretinus

I will blend
My cruelty with some scorn, or else 'tis lost;
Revenge, when it is unexpected, falling
With greater violence; and hate cloth'd in smiles
Strikes, and with horror, dead the wretch that comes not
Prepar'd to meet it.

Enter Lamia with the Guard

Our good Lamia, welcome!
So much we owe you for a benefit
With willingness on your part conferr'd upon us.

Lamia   'Tis beneath your fate
To be oblig'd, that in your own hand grasp
The means to be magnificent.

Caesar   Well put off;
But yet it must not do. The empire, Lamia,
Divided equally, can hold no weight
If balanc'd with your gift in fair Domitia.
You that could part with all delights at once,
The magazine of rich pleasures being contain'd
In her perfections, uncompell'd, deliver'd
As a present fit for Caesar; in your eyes

With tears of joy, not sorrow, 'tis confirm'd
You glory in your act.

Lamia   Derided too!
Sir, this is more –

Caesar   More than I can requite:
It is acknowledg'd, Lamia. There's no drop
Of melting nectar I taste from her lip
But yields a touch of immortality
To the blest receiver; every grace and feature,
Priz'd to the worth, bought at an easy rate
If purchas'd for a consulship. Her discourse
So ravishing, and her action so attractive,
That I would part with all my other senses,
Provided I might ever see and hear her.
The pleasures of her bed I dare not trust
The winds or air with, for that would draw down
In envy of my happiness, a war
From all the gods upon me.

Lamia   Your compassion
To me in your forbearing to insult
On my calamity, which you make your sport,
Would more appease those gods you have provok'd
Than all the blasphemous comparisons
You sing unto her praise.

Caesar   I sing her praise?
'Tis far from my ambition to hope it,
It being a debt she only can lay down,
And no tongue else discharge.

Music above and a song

Hark! I think, prompted
With my consent that you once more should hear her,
She does begin. – An universal silence

Dwell on this place! 'Tis death with ling'ring torments
To all that dare disturb her.

The song ended, Caesar goes on.

Who can hear this
And falls not down and worships? Say, Lamia, say,
Is not her voice angelical?

Lamia   To your ear;
But I, alas, am silent.

Caesar   Be so ever.
And in thy hope, or wish, to repossess
What I love more than empire, I pronounce thee
Guilty of treason. – Off with his head! Do you stare?
By her that is my patroness, Minerva
(Whose statue I adore of all the gods),
If he but live to make reply, thy life
Shall answer it!

The Guard lead off Lamia, stopping his mouth.

My fears of him are freed now,
And he that liv'd to upbraid me with my wrong,
For an offence he never could imagine,
In wantonness remov'd.
[*To Domitia*]   Descend, my dearest.
Plurality of husbands shall no more
Breed doubts or jealousies in you. 'Tis dispatch'd,
And with as little trouble here as if
I had kill'd a fly.

*Enter Domitia, ushered in by Aretinus, her train with all state
borne up by Julia, Caenis and Domitilla*

Now you appear, and in
That glory you deserve, and these that stoop
To do you service in the act much honour'd.

Julia, forget that Titus was thy father;
Caenis and Domitilla, ne'er remember
Sabinus or Vespasian. To be slaves
To her is more true liberty than to live
Parthian or Asian queens. Thus I seat you
By Caesar's side – commanding these, that once
Were the adored glories of the time
(To witness to the world they are your vassals)
At your feet to attend you.

Domitia
                'Tis your pleasure,
And not my pride. And yet when I consider
That I am yours, all duties they can pay
I do receive as circumstances due
To her you please to honour.

       Enter Parthenius, with Philargus

Parthenius
                Caesar's will
Commands you hither, nor must you gainsay it.

Philargus
Lose time to see an interlude? Must I pay too
For my vexation?

Parthenius
             Not in the court;
It is the emperor's charge.

Philargus
              I shall endure
My torment then the better.

Caesar
              Can it be
This sordid thing, Parthenius, is thy father?
No actor can express him. I had held
The fiction for impossible in the scene,
Had I not seen the substance. – Sirrah, sit still,
And give attention; if you but nod
You sleep for ever. – Let them spare the prologue,
And all the ceremonies proper to ourself,
And come to the last act, there where the cure

> By the doctor is made perfect. – The swift minutes
> Seem years to me, Domitia, that divorce thee
> From my embraces. My desires increasing
> As they are satisfied, all pleasures else
> Are tedious as dull sorrows. Kiss me; again.
> If I now wanted heat of youth, these fires
> In Priam's veins would thaw his frozen blood,
> Enabling him to get a second Hector
> For the defence of Troy.

Domitia   You are wanton!
> Pray you forbear. Let me see the play.

Caesar   Begin there.

Enter Paris like a Doctor of Physic, Aesopus as the son.
Latinus brought forth asleep in a chair, a key in his mouth.

Aesopus   O master doctor, he is past recovery;
> A lethargy hath seiz'd him, and however
> His sleep resemble death, his watchful care
> To guard that treasure he dares make no use of
> Works strongly in his soul.

Paris   What's that he holds
> So fast between his teeth?

Aesopus   The key that opens
> His iron chests, cramm'd with accursed gold,
> Rusty with long imprisonment. There's no duty
> In me, his son, nor confidence in friends,
> That can persuade him to deliver up
> That to the trust of any.

Philargus   He is the wiser;
> We were fashion'd in one mould.

Aesopus   He eats with it;
> And when devotion calls him to the Temple
> Of Mammon, whom of all the gods he kneels to,

That held thus still, his orisons are paid;
Nor will he, though the wealth of Rome were pawn'd
For the restoring of it, for one short hour
Be won to part with it.

Paris   I'll try if I can force it.
It will not be. His avaricious mind
(Like men in rivers drown'd) makes him gripe fast
To his last gasp.

Aesopus   Is he not dead?

Paris   You may with safety pinch him,
Or under his nails stick needles, yet he stirs not;
Anxious fear to lose what his soul dotes on
Renders his flesh insensible. We must use
Some means to rouse the sleeping faculties
Of his mind. Take a trumpet
And blow it in his ears; 'tis to no purpose.
And yet despair not; I have one trick left.

Aesopus   What is it?

Paris   I will cause a fearful dream
To steal into his fancy, and so free his body's organs.

Domitia   'Tis a cunning fellow!
If he were indeed a doctor, as the play says,
He should be sworn my servant, govern my slumbers,
And minister to me waking.

                                        A chest brought in

Paris   If this fail
I'll give him o'er. So, with all violence
Rend ope this iron chest. Louder yet!
'Tis open, and already he begins
To stir; mark with what trouble.

                                        Latinus stretches himself

Philargus	As you are Caesar,
	Defend this honest, thrifty man! They are thieves,
	And come to rob him.
Parthenius	Peace! The emperor frowns.
Paris	So; now pour out the bags upon the table;
	Remove his jewels, and his bonds. Once more.
Latinus	Murder! Murder!
	They come to murder me! My son in the plot?
	Oh thee, that dost assassinate my soul!
	My gold! my bonds! my jewels! Dost thou envy
	My glad possession of them for a day?
	Thou worse than parricide!
Paris	Seem not to mind him.
Latinus	Have I, to leave thee rich, denied myself
	The joys of human being; scrap'd and hoarded
	A mass of treasure? And to save expense
	In outward ornaments, I did expose
	My naked body to the winter's cold,
	And summer's scorching heat. Nay, when diseases
	Grew thick upon me, and a little cost
	Had purchas'd my recovery, I chose rather
	To have my ashes clos'd up in my urn
	By hasting on my fate than to diminish
	The gold my prodigal son, while I am living,
	Carelessly scatters.
Aesopus	Would you would dispatch and die once.
	Your ghost should feel in hell, that is my slave
	Which was your master.
Philargus	Out upon thee, varlet!
Paris	And what then follows all your cark, and caring,
	And self-affliction, when your starv'd trunk is
	Turn'd to forgotten dust? This hopeful youth

Urines upon your monument, ne'er rememb'ring
How much for him you suffer'd; and then feasts
His senses all at once – a happiness
You never granted to yourself. Your gold, then,
Got with vexation, and preserv'd with trouble,
Maintains the public stews, panders and ruffians
That quaff damnations to your memory
For living so long here.

Latinus   'Twill be so, I see it.
Oh, that I could redeem the time that's past!

Paris   Covetous men,
Having one foot in the grave, lament so ever.
But grant that I by art could restore your body
To perfect health; will you with care endeavour
To rectify your mind?

Latinus   I should so live then
As neither my heir should have just cause to think
I liv'd too long, for being close-handed to him,
Or cruel to myself.

Paris   Have your desires.
Phoebus assisting me, I will repair
The ruin'd building of your health; and think not
You have a son that hates you. The truth is,
This means, with his consent, I practis'd on you
To this good end: it being a device
In you to show *The Cure of Avarice.*

                          Exeunt Paris, Latinus, Aesopus

Philargus   An old fool to be gull'd thus! Had he died
As I resolve to do, not to be alter'd,
It had gone off twanging.

Caesar   How approve you, sweetest,
Of the matter and the actors?

Domitia
                                        For the subject,
I like it not; it was filch'd out of Horace
– Nay, I have read the poets – but the fellow
That play'd the doctor did it well, by Venus!
He had a tuneable tongue and neat delivery;
And yet in my opinion he would perform
A lover's part much better. Prithee, Caesar,
For I grow weary, let us see tomorrow
Iphis and Anaxerete.

Caesar
                                        Anything
For thy delight, Domitia. To your rest
Till I come to disquiet you. – Wait upon her. –
There is a business I must dispatch,
And I will straight be with you.

                    Exeunt Aretinus, Domitia, Julia, Caenis, Domitilla

Parthenius
                                        Now, my dread sir,
Endeavour to prevail.

Caesar
                                        One way or other
We'll cure him, never doubt it. – Now, Philargus,
Thou wretched thing, dost thou in thyself
Feel true compunction, with a resolution
To be a new man?

Philargus
                                This craz'd body's Caesar's,
But for my mind –

Caesar
                                Trifle not with my anger.
Canst thou make good use of what was now presented?
And imitate in thy sudden change of life
The miserable rich man that express'd
What thou art to the life?

Philargus
                                        Pray you, give me leave
To die as I have liv'd. I must not part with
My gold; it is my life. I am past cure.

Caesar   No! By Minerva, thou shalt never more
                    Feel the least touch of avarice. Take him hence
                    And hang him instantly. If there be gold in hell,
                    Enjoy it; thine here and thy life together
                    Is forfeited.

Philargus   Was I sent for to this purpose?

Parthenius   Mercy for all my service, Caesar, mercy!

Caesar   Should Jove plead for him, 'tis resolv'd he dies,
                    And he that speaks one syllable to dissuade me;
                    And therefore tempt me not. It is but justice.

                                                        Exeunt

ACT THREE

SCENE ONE

Enter Julia, Domitilla, Stephanos

Julia	No, Domitilla; if you but compare What I have suffer'd with your injuries (Though great ones, I confess), they will appear Like molehills to Olympus.
Domitilla	You are tender Of your own wounds, which makes you lose the feeling And sense of mine. The incest he committed With you, he won by his perjuries that he would Salute you with the title of Augusta. Your faint denial show'd a full consent And grant to his temptations. But poor I, That would not yield, but was with violence forc'd To serve his lusts, and in a kind Tiberius At Caprae never practis'd, have not here One conscious touch to rise up my accuser, I in my will being innocent.
Stephanos	Pardon me, Great princesses, though I presume to tell you, There is something more in Rome expected From Titus' daughter and his uncle's heir Than womanish complaints after such wrongs, Which mercy cannot pardon. But you'll say Your hands are weak, and should you but attempt A just revenge on this inhuman monster, This prodigy of mankind, bloody Domitian, Hath ready swords at his command, as well

As islands to confine you, to remove
His doubts and fears, did he but entertain
The least suspicion.

Julia   'Tis true, Stephanos.
The legions that sack'd Jerusalem
Under my father Titus are sworn his,
And I no more remember'd.

Domitilla   And to lose
Ourselves by building on impossible hopes
Were desperate madness.

Stephanos   You conclude too fast.
One single arm, whose master does contemn
His own life, holds a full command o'er his,
Spite of his guards. I was your bondman, lady,
And you my gracious patroness; my wealth
And liberty your gift; and though no soldier,
To whom or custom or example makes
Grim death appear less terrible, I dare die
To do you service. Say but you, 'Go on!'
And I will reach his heart, or perish in
The noble undertaking.

Domitilla   I must not
Upon uncertain grounds hazard so grateful
And good a servant. The immortal powers
Protect a prince, though sold to impious acts,
And seem to slumber till his roaring crimes
Awake their justice; but then looking down,
They in their secret judgements do determine
To leave him to his wickedness, which sinks him
When he is most secure.

Julia   His cruelty
Increasing daily, of necessity
Must render him as odious to his soldiers,

Familiar friends, and freemen, as it hath done
Already to the Senate; then, forsaken
Of his supporters, and grown terrible
E'en to himself, and her he now so dotes on,
We may put into act what now with safety
We cannot whisper.

Stephanos   I am still prepar'd
To execute when you please to command me.

Enter Caenis

Julia   Oh, here's Caenis.

Domitilla   Whence come you?

Caenis   From the empress, who seems mov'd
In that you wait no better. Her pride's grown
To such a height that she disdains the service
Of her own women, and esteems herself
Neglected when the princesses of the blood
On every coarse employment are not ready
To stoop to her commands.

Domitilla   Where is her greatness?

Caenis   Where you would little think she could descend
To grace the room or persons.

Julia   Speak; where is she?

Caenis   Among the players; where all state laid by,
She does inquire who acts this part, who that,
And in what habits; blames the tire-women
For want of curious dressings; and so taken
She is with Paris the tragedian's shape,
That is to act a lover, I thought once
She would have courted him.

Domitilla   In the meantime
How spends the emperor his hours?

Caenis	As ever.
	And but this morning (if't be possible)
	He hath outgone himself, having condemn'd
	At Aretinus his informer's suit,
	Palphurius Sura and good Junius Rusticus,
	Men of the best repute in Rome for their
	Integrity of life; no fault objected,
	But that they did lament his cruel sentence
	On Paetus Thrasea the philosopher,
	Their patron and instructor.

Caenis   As ever.
And but this morning (if't be possible)
He hath outgone himself, having condemn'd
At Aretinus his informer's suit,
Palphurius Sura and good Junius Rusticus,
Men of the best repute in Rome for their
Integrity of life; no fault objected,
But that they did lament his cruel sentence
On Paetus Thrasea the philosopher,
Their patron and instructor.

Stephanos   Can Jove see this,
And hold his thunder!

Domitilla   Nero and Caligula
Commanded only mischiefs; but our Caesar
Delights to see 'em.

Julia   What we cannot help,
We may deplore with silence.

Caenis   We are call'd for
By our proud mistress.

Domitilla   We a while must suffer.

Stephanos   It is true fortitude to stand firm against
All shocks of fate, when cowards faint and die
In fear to suffer more calamity.

                                                        Exeunt

SCENE TWO

Enter Caesar, Parthenius

Caesar   They are then in fetters?

Parthenius   Yes, sir, but –

Caesar   I'll have thy thoughts. Deliver them.

Parthenius   I shall, sir.
But still submitting to your god-like pleasure
Which cannot be instructed –

Caesar   To the point.

Parthenius   Nor let your sacred majesty believe
Your vassal, that with dry eyes look'd upon
His father dragg'd to death by your command,
Can pity these, that durst presume to censure
What you decreed.

Caesar   Well? Forward.

Parthenius   Alas, I know, sir,
These bookmen, Rusticus and Palphurius Sura,
Deserve all tortures. Yet, in my opinion,
They being popular senators, and cried up
With loud applauses of the multitude
For foolish honesty and beggarly virtue,
'Twould relish more of policy to have them
Made away in private, with what exquisite torments
You please – it skills not – than to have them drawn
To the degrees in public; for 'tis doubted
That the sad object may beget compassion
In the giddy rout, and cause some sudden uproar
That may disturb you.

Caesar   Hence, pale-spirited coward!

> Can we descend so far beneath ourself
> As or to court the people's love, or fear
> Their worst of hate? Can they, that are as dust
> Before the whirlwind of our will and power,
> Add any moment to us? Or thou think,
> If there are gods above, or goddesses
> (But wise Minerva that's mine own and sure),
> That they have vacant hours to take into
> Their serious protection or care
> This many-headed monster, the people!
> Bring forth those condemn'd wretches. Let me see
> One man so lost as but to pity 'em,
> And though there lay a million of souls
> Imprison'd in his flesh, my hangmen's hooks
> Should rend it off and give 'em liberty.
> Caesar hath said it.

Exit Parthenius

Enter Parthenius, Aretinus, and the Guard; Hangmen
dragging in Junius Rusticus and Palphurius Sura, bound back to back.

Aretinus	[*To the Guard*] 'Tis great Caesar's pleasure That with fix'd eyes you carefully observe The people's looks. Charge upon any man That with sigh, or murmur, does express A seeming sorrow for these traitors' deaths. You know his will, perform it.
Caesar	A good bloodhound, And fit for my employments.
Sura	Give us leave To die, fell tyrant.
Rusticus	For beyond our bodies Thou hast no power.
Caesar	Yes; I'll afflict your souls, And force them groaning to the Stygian lake,

Prepar'd for such to howl in that blaspheme
The power of princes, that are gods on earth.
Tremble to think how terrible the dream is
After this sleep of death.

Rusticus   To guilty men
It may bring terror; not to us, that know
What 'tis to die, well taught by his example
For whom we suffer. In my thought I see
The substance of that pure untainted soul
Of Thrasea our master, made a star,
That with melodious harmony invites us
(Leaving this dunghill Rome, made hell by thee)
To trace his heavenly steps.

Caesar   Do invoke him
With all the aids his sanctity of life
Have won on the rewarders of his virtue,
They shall not save you. Dogs, do you grin? Torment 'em.

The Hangmen torment 'em, they still smiling

Again, again! You trifle. Not a groan!
Is my rage lost? What cursed charms defend 'em!
Search deeper, villains! Who looks pale? Or thinks
That I am cruel?

Aretinus   Over-merciful.
'Tis all your weakness, sir.

Parthenius   [*Aside*]   I dare not show
A sign of sorrow; yet my sinews shrink,
The spectacle is so horrid.

Caesar   I was never
O'ercome till now. For my sake roar a little,
And show you are corporeal, and not turn'd
Aerial spirits. Will it not do? I am tortur'd
In their want of feeling torments. Are they not dead?

Sura   No, we live.

Rusticus   Live to deride thee, our calm patience treading
                Upon the neck of tyranny. That securely
                (As 'twere a gentle slumber) we endure
                Thy hangman's studied tortures, is a debt
                We owe to grave philosophy, that instructs us
                The flesh is but the clothing of the soul,
                Which growing out of fashion, though it be
                Cast off, or rent, or torn, like ours, 'tis then,
                Being itself divine, in her best lustre.
                But unto such as thou, that have no hopes
                Beyond the present, every little scar,
                The want of rest, excess of heat or cold,
                That does inform them only they are mortal,
                Pierce through and through them.

Caesar   We will hear no more.

Rusticus   This only, and I give thee warning of it.
                Though it is in thy will to grind this earth
                As small as atoms, they thrown in the sea too,
                They shall seem re-collected to thy sense;
                And when the sandy building of thy greatness
                Shall with its own weight totter, look to see me
                As I was yesterday, in my perfect shape,
                For I'll appear in horror.

Caesar   By my shaking,
                I am the guilty man, and not the judge.
                Drag from my sight these cursed ominous wizards.
                Away with 'em! First show them death, then leave
                No memory of their ashes. I'll mock fate.

                            Exeunt Hangmen with Rusticus and Sura

                Shall words fright him, victorious armies circle?
                No, no the fever does begin to leave me.

Enter Domitia, Julia, Caenis, Stephanos following

Or, were it deadly, from this living fountain
I could renew the vigour of my youth,
Oh my glory! My life! Command! My all!

Domitia   As you to me are.

Embracing and kissing mutually

I heard you were sad; I have prepar'd you sport
Will banish melancholy. Sirrah, Caesar,
(I hug myself for't) I have been instructing
The players how to act, and to cut off
All tedious impertinency, have contracted
The tragedy into one continu'd scene.
I have the art of't, and am taken more
With my ability that way than all knowledge
I have but of thy love.

Caesar   Thou art still thyself;
The sweetest, wittiest –

Domitia   When we are a-bed
I'll thank your good opinion. Thou shalt see
Such an Iphis of thy Paris! And to humble
The pride of Domitilla that neglects me,
I have forc'd her to the part of Anaxarete.
You are not offended with it?

Caesar   Anything
That does content thee yields delight to me.
My faculties and powers are thine.

Domitia   I thank you.
Prithee let's take our places. Bid 'em enter
Without more circumstance.

They sit

After a short flourish, enter Paris as Iphis

                    How do you like
That shape? Methinks it is most suitable
To the aspect of a despairing lover.
The seeming late-fall'n, counterfeited tears
That hang upon his cheeks was my device.

Caesar   And all was excellent.

Domitia   Now hear him speak.

Paris   That she is fair (and that an epithet
Too foul to express her), or descended nobly,
Or rich, or fortunate, are certain truths
In which poor Iphis glories. But that these
Perfections, in no other virgin found,
Abus'd, should nourish cruelty and pride
In the divinest Anaxarete,
Is, to my love-sick, languishing soul, a riddle.
Imperious Love,
As at thy ever-flaming altars Iphis,
Thy never-tired votary, hath presented
With scalding tears whole hecatombs of sighs,
Preferring thy power, be auspicious
To this last trial of my sacrifice
Of love and service!

Domitia   Does he not act it rarely?
Observe with what a feeling he delivers
His orisons to Cupid. I am rapt with't.

Paris   And from thy never-emptied quiver take
A golden arrow, to transfix her heart
And force her love like me, or cure my wound
With a leaden one, that may beget in me
Hate and forgetfulness of what's now my idol.
With my glad lips I kiss this earth, grown proud
With frequent favours from her delicate feet.

Domitia	By Caesar's life, he weeps! And I forbear Hardly to keep him company.
Paris	Within there, ho! Something divine, come forth To a distressed mortal! *Knocks*

Enter Latinus as a porter.

Latinus	Ha! Who knocks there?
Domitia	What a churlish look this knave has!
Latinus	Is't you, sirrah? Are you come to pule and whine? Avaunt, and quickly! Dog-whips shall drive you hence else.
Domitia	Churlish devil! But that I should disturb the scene, as I live I would tear his eyes out.
Caesar	'Tis in jest, Domitia.
Domitia	I do not like such jesting; if he were not A flinty-hearted slave, he could not use One of his form so harshly. How the toad swells At the other's sweet humility!
Caesar	'Tis his part; Let 'em proceed.
Domitia	A rogue's part; will ne'er leave him.
Paris	[*Kneels*] Scorn not your servant, that with suppliant hands Takes hold upon your knees, conjuring you As you are a man, and did not suck the milk Of wolves and tigers, or a mother of A tougher temper, use some means these eyes, Before they are wept out, may see your lady. Will you be gracious, sir?
Latinus	Though I lose my place for't I can hold out no longer.

Domitia	Now he melts There is some little hope he may die honest.
Latinus	Madam!

Enter Domitilla for Anaxarete

Domitilla	Who calls? What object have we here?
Domitia	Your cousin keeps her proud state still; I think I have fitted her for a part.
Domitilla	Did I not charge thee I ne'er might see this thing more?
Paris	I am indeed What thing you please, a worm that you may tread on. Lower I cannot fall to show my duty.
Domitilla	What dull fool But thou could nourish any flattering hope One of my height in youth, in birth and fortune, Could e'er descend to look upon thy lowness? Much less consent to make my lord of one I'd not accept, though offer'd for my slave. My thoughts stoop not so low.
Domitia	That's her true nature, No personated scorn.
Domitilla	I wrong my worth Or to exchange a syllable or look With one so far beneath me.
Paris	Yet take heed, Take heed of pride, and curiously consider How brittle the foundation is, on which You labour to advance it. The love I bring you Nor time, nor sickness, violent thieves, nor fate, Can ravish from you.

Domitia   Could the oracle
            Give better counsel!

Paris   Say will you relent yet,
            Revoking your decree that I should die?
            Or shall I do what you command? Resolve;
            I am impatient of delay.

Domitilla   Dispatch then.
            I shall look on your tragedy unmov'd,
            Peradventure laugh at it, for it will prove
            A comedy to me.

Domitia   Oh devil! Devil!

Paris   Then thus I take my last leave. All the curses
            Of lovers fall upon you; and hereafter
            When any man, like me contemn'd, shall study
            In the anguish of his soul to give a name
            To a scornful, cruel mistress, let him only
            Say, 'This most bloody woman is to me
            As Anaxarete was to wretched Iphis!'
            Now feast your tyrannous mind, and glory in
            The ruins you have made. For Hymen's bands

                                    Produces a noose

            That should have made us one, this fatal halter
            For ever shall divorce us; at your gate,
            As a trophy of your pride, and my affliction,
            I'll presently hang myself.

Domitia   [*Rises*]   Not for the world!
            Restrain him, as you love your lives!

Caesar   Why are you
            Transported thus, Domitia? 'Tis a play;
            Or grant it serious, it at no part merits
            This passion in you.

Paris

I ne'er purpos'd, madam,
To do the deed in earnest, though I bow
To your care and tenderness of me.

Domitia

Let me, sir,
Entreat your pardon; what I saw presented
Carried me beyond myself.

Caesar

To your place again,
And see what follows.

Domitia

No, I am familiar
With the conclusion; besides, upon the sudden
I feel myself much indispos'd.

Caesar

To bed then;
I'll be thy doctor.

Aretinus

[*Aside*] There is something more
In this than passion, which I must find out,
Or my intelligence freezes.

Domitia

Come to me, Paris,
Tomorrow, for your reward.

Exeunt all but Domitilla and Stephanos

Stephanos

Patroness, hear me!
Will you not call for your share?

Domitilla

Prithee be patient.
I that have suffer'd greater wrongs bear this;
And that, till my revenge, my comfort is.

Exeunt

ACT FOUR

SCENE ONE

Enter Parthenius, Julia, Domitilla, Caenis

Parthenius	Why, 'tis impossible! Paris?
Julia	You observ'd not The violence of her passion, when he pretended (For your contempt, fair Anaxarete) To hang himself.
Parthenius	Yes, yes, I noted that; But never could imagine it could work her To such a strange intemperance of affection As to dote on him.
Domitilla	By my hopes, I think That she respects not, though all here saw and mark'd it, Presuming she can mould the emperor's will Into what form she likes, though we, and all Th'informers of the world, conspir'd to cross it.
Caenis	Then with what eagerness, this morning, urging The want of health and rest, she did entreat Caesar to leave her.
Domitilla	Who no sooner absent But she calls, 'Dwarf!' (so in her scorn she styles me) 'Put on my pantofles; fetch pen and paper, I am to write'; and with distracted looks, In her smock, impatient of so short delay, She seal'd I know not what, but 'twas endors'd 'To my lov'd Paris'.

Julia   Add to this, I heard her
Say, when a page receiv'd it, 'Let him wait me,
And carefully, in the walk call'd our retreat,
Where Caesar, in his fear to give offence,
Unsent for never enters.'

Parthenius   This being certain,
Why do not you that are so near in blood
Discover it?

Domitilla   Alas, you know we dare not.
'Twill be receiv'd for a malicious practice
To free us from that slavery which her pride
Imposes on us. But if you would please
To break the ice, on pain to be sunk ever,
We would aver it.

Parthenius   I would second you,
But that I am commanded with all speed
To fetch in Ascletario the Chaldaean,
Who in his absence is condemn'd of treason
For calculating the nativity
Of Caesar, with all confidence foretelling
In every circumstance when he shall die
A violent death. Yet, if you could approve
Of my directions, I would have you speak
As much to Aretinus as you have
To me deliver'd. He in his own nature
Being a spy, on weaker grounds, no doubt,
Will undertake it; not for goodness' sake
(With which he never yet held correspondence),
But to triumph in the ruins of this Paris,
That cross'd him in the Senate-house.

                    Enter Aretinus

                                  Here he comes,
His nose held up; he hath something in the wind,

Or I much err, already. My designs
Command me hence, great ladies, but I leave
My wishes with you.

Exit Parthenius

Aretinus   Have I caught your greatness
In the trap, my proud Augusta!

Domitilla   What is't raps him?

Aretinus   And my fine Roman actor! Is't even so?
No coarser dish to take your wanton palate
Save that which, but the emperor, none durst taste of?
'Tis very well. I needs must glory in
This rare discovery.

Domitilla   This is more
Than usual with him.

Julia   Aretinus!

Aretinus   How?
No more respect and reverence tender'd to me
But 'Aretinus'! 'Tis confess'd that title,
When you were princesses, and commanded all,
Had been a favour; but being, as you are,
Vassals to a proud woman (the worst bondage),
You stand oblig'd with as much adoration
To entertain him that comes arm'd with strength
To break your fetters, as tann'd galley-slaves
Pay such as do redeem them from the oar.
I come not to entrap you, but aloud
Pronounce that you are manumis'd; and to make
Your liberty sweeter, you shall see her fall
(This empress, this Domitia, what you will)
That triumph'd in your miseries.

Domitilla   Were you serious,

To prove your accusation I could lend
Some help.

Caenis   And I.

Julia   And I.

Aretinus   No atom to me.
My eyes and ears are everywhere; I know all,
To the line and action in the play that took her;
Her quick dissimulation to excuse
Her being transported, with her morning passion.
I brib'd the boy that did convey the letter,
And having perus'd it, made it up again.
Your griefs and angers are to me familiar;
That Paris is brought to her, and how far
He shall be tempted.

Domitilla   This is above wonder.

Aretinus   My gold can work much stranger miracles
Than to corrupt poor waiters. Here, join with me –

Offers a paper

'Tis a complaint to Caesar. This is that
Shall ruin her, and raise you. Have you set your hands
To the accusation?

The women sign the paper

Julia   And will justify
What we have subscrib'd to.

Caenis   And with vehemency.

Domitilla   I will deliver it.

Aretinus   Leave the rest to me then.

Enter Caesar with his Guard.

Aretinus   Caesar!

Julia	As thou art More than a man –
Caenis	Let not thy passions be Rebellious to thy reason –

The petition deliver'd by Domitilla

Domitilla	But receive This trial of your constancy as unmov'd As you go to or from the Capitol, Thanks given to Jove for triumphs.
Caesar	Ha!
Domitilla	Vouchsafe A while to stay the lightning of your eyes Poor mortals dare not look on.
Aretinus	There's no vein Of yours that rises high with rage, but is An earthquake to us.
Domitilla	And if kept not clos'd With more than human patience, in a moment Will swallow us to the centre.
Caenis	Not that we Repine to serve her, are we her accusers.
Julia	But that she's fall'n so low.
Aretinus	Which on sure proofs We can make good.
Domitilla	And show she is unworthy Of the least spark of that diviner fire You have conferr'd upon her.
Caesar	I stand doubtful And unresolv'd what to determine of you. In this malicious violence you have offer'd

To the altar of her truth, and pureness to me,
You have but fruitlessly labour'd to sully
A white robe of perfection black-mouth'd envy
Could belch no spot on. But I will put off
The deity you labour to take from me,
And argue out of probabilities with you,
As if I were a man. Can I believe
That she that borrows all her light from me,
And knows to use it, would betray her darkness
To you that are her slaves, and therefore hate her,
Whose aids she might employ to make way for her?
Or Aretinus, whom long since she knew
To be the cabinet counsellor, nay, the key,
Of Caesar's secrets? Could her beauty raise her
To this unequall'd height, to make her fall
The more remarkable?
Or she leave our imperial bed to court
A public actor?

Aretinus   Who dares contradict
These more than human reasons, that have power
To clothe base guilt in the most glorious shape
Of innocence?

Domitilla   Too well she knew the strength
And eloquence of her patron to defend her,
And thereupon presuming, fell securely,
Not fearing an accuser.

Caesar   I'll not hear
A syllable more that may invite a change
In my opinion of her. You have rais'd
A fiercer war within me by this fable
(Though with your lives you vow to make it history)
Than if, and at one instant, all my legions
Revolted from me, and came arm'd against me.
Here in this paper are the swords predestin'd
For my destruction; here the fatal stars

That threaten more than ruin; this the death's head
That does assure me, if she can prove false,
That I am mortal, which a sudden fever
Would prompt me to believe, and faintly yield to.
But now in my full confidence what she suffers,
In that, from any witness but myself,
I nourish a suspicion she's untrue,
My toughness returns to me. Lead on, monsters,
And by the forfeit of your lives confirm
She is all excellence, as you all baseness;
Or let mankind, for her fall, boldly swear
There are no chaste wives now, nor ever were.

Exeunt

SCENE TWO

Enter Domitia, Paris, Servants.

Domitia   Say we command that none presume to dare,
On forfeit of our favour, that is life,
Out of a saucy curiousness to stand
Within the distance of their eyes or ears
Till we please to be waited on.

Exeunt Servants

                      And, sirrah,
Howe'er you are excepted, let it not
Beget in you an arrogant opinion
'Tis done to grace you.

Paris   With my humblest service
I but obey your summons, and should blush else
To be so near you.

Domitia   'Twould become you rather
To fear the greatness of the grace vouchsaf'd you
May overwhelm you; and 'twill do no less
If, when you are rewarded, in your cups
You boast this privacy.

Paris   That were, mightiest empress,
To play with lightning.

Domitia   You conceive it right.
The means to kill, or save, is not alone
In Caesar circumscrib'd, for if incens'd
We have our thunder too, that strikes as deadly.

Paris   'Twould ill become the lowness of my fortune
To question what you can do, but with all
Humility to attend what is your will,
And then to serve it.

Domitia   And would not a secret
(Suppose we should commit it to your trust)
Scald you to keep it?

Paris   Though it rag'd within me
Till I turn'd cinders, it should ne'er have vent.
To be an age a-dying, and with torture,
Only to be thought worthy of your counsel
Were a perpetual happiness.

Domitia   We could wish
That we could credit thee, and cannot find
In reason but that thou, whom oft I have seen
To personate a gentleman, noble, wise,
Faithful, and gamesome, and what virtues else
The poet pleases to adorn you with,
But that (as vessels still partake the odour
Of the sweet, precious liquors they contain'd)
Thou must be really, in some degree,
The thing thou dost present. Nay, do not tremble.

We seriously believe it, and presume
Our Paris is the volume in which all
Those excellent gifts the stage hath seen him grac'd with
Are curiously bound up.

Paris   The argument
Is the same, great Augusta, that I acting
A fool, a coward, a traitor, or cold cynic,
Or any other weak and vicious person,
Of force I must be such. O gracious madam,
How glorious soever, or deform'd,
I do appear in the scene, my part being ended,
And all my borrow'd ornaments put off,
I am no more nor less than what I was
Before I enter'd.

Domitia   Come, you would put on
A wilful ignorance, and not understand
What 'tis we point at. Must we in plain language,
Against the decent modesty of our sex,
Say that we love thee, love thee to enjoy thee,
Or that in our desires thou art preferr'd,
And Caesar but thy second?

Paris   O madam, hear me with a patient ear,
And be but pleas'd to understand the reasons
That do deter me from a happiness
Kings would be rivals for. Can I, that owe
My life and all that's mine to Caesar's bounties,
Make payment for them with ingratitude,
Falsehood, and treason? Though you have a shape
Might tempt Hippolytus, and larger power
To help, or hurt, than wanton Phaedra had,
Let loyalty and duty plead my pardon,
Though I refuse to satisfy.

Domitia   You are coy,
Expecting I should court you. Let mean ladies

Use prayers and entreaties to their creatures
To rise up instruments to serve their pleasures;
But for Augusta so to lose herself,
That holds command o'er Caesar and the world,
Were poverty of spirit. Thou must! Thou shalt!
The violence of my passions knows no mean,
I'll use no moderation. Take this only
As a caution from me: threadbare chastity
Is poor in the advancement of her servants,
But wantonness magnificent; and 'tis frequent
To have the salary of vice weigh down
The pay of virtue. So, without more trifling,
Thy sudden answer.

Paris   [*Aside*]   In what a strait I am brought in!
Alas! I know that the denial's death,
Nor can my grant, discover'd, threaten more.
Yet to die innocent, and have the glory
For all posterity to report that I
Refus'd an empress to preserve my faith
To my great master, in true judgement must
Show fairer than to buy a guilty life
With wealth and honours. 'Tis the base I build on. –
I dare not, must not, will not.

Domitia   How! Contemn'd?
[*Aside*] Since hopes nor fears in the extremes prevail not,
I must use a mean. – Think who 'tis sues to thee.
Deny not that yet which a brother may
Grant to his sister. As a testimony

Enter above Caesar, Aretinus, Julia, Domitilla, Caenis

I am not scorn'd, kiss me. Kiss me again.
Kiss closer. Thou art now my Trojan Paris,
And I thy Helen.

Paris   Since it is your will.

Caesar	And I am Menelaus. But I shall be Something I know not yet.

Caesar descends

Domitia	Why lose we time And opportunity? These are but salads To sharpen appetite. Let us to the feast,

Courting Paris wantonly

Where I shall wish that thou wert Jupiter,
And I Alcmena, and that I had power
To lengthen out one short night into three,
And so beget a Hercules.

Enter Caesar and Guard

Caesar	While Amphitrio Stands by, and draws the curtains.

Paris	Oh!

Falls on his face

Domitia	Betray'd?

Caesar	No; taken in a net of Vulcan's filing, Where, in myself, the theatre of the gods Are sad spectators, not one of them daring To witness with a smile he does desire To be so sham'd for all the pleasure that You have sold your being for. What shall I name thee? Ingrateful, treacherous, insatiate, all Invectives which in bitterness of spirit Wrong'd men have breath'd out against wicked women, Cannot express thee. Have I rais'd thee from Thy low condition to the height of greatness, Command, and majesty, in one base act To render me, that was (before I hugg'd thee, An adder, to my bosom) more than a man,

A thing beneath a beast? Am I thus rewarded?
Not a knee? Nor tear? Nor sign of sorrow for thy fault?
Break, stubborn silence! What canst thou allege
To stay my vengeance?

Domitia   This. Thy lust compell'd me
To be a strumpet, and mine hath return'd it
In my intent and will (though not in act)
To cuckold thee.

Caesar   O impudence! Take her hence,
And let her make her entrance into hell
By leaving life with all the tortures that
Flesh can be sensible of. Yet stay. What power
Her beauty still holds o'er my soul, that wrongs
Of this unpardonable nature cannot teach me
To right myself and hate her! – Kill her! – Hold!
Oh, that my dotage should increase from that
Which should breed detestation. By Minerva,
If I look on her longer, I shall melt
And sue to her, my injuries forgot,
Again to be receiv'd into her favour,
Could honour yield to it! Carry her to her chamber;
Be that her prison till in cooler blood
I shall determine of her.

Exit Guard with Domitia

Aretinus   [*Aside*]   Now step I in,
While he's in this calm mood, for my reward. –
Sir, if my service hath deserv'd –

Caesar   Yes, yes;
And I'll reward thee. Thou hast robb'd me of
All rest and peace, and been the principal means
To make me know that, of which if again

Enter Guard

I could be ignorant of, I would purchase it
With loss of empire. – Strangle him; take these hence too
And lodge them in the dungeon. – Could your reason,
Dull wretches, flatter you with hope to think
That this discovery, that hath shower'd upon me
Perpetual vexation, should not fall
Heavy on you? – Away with 'em! Stop their mouths;
I will hear no reply.

Exeunt Guard, Aretinus, Julia, Caenis, and Domitilla

     O Paris, Paris,
How shall I argue with thee? How begin
To make thee understand, before I kill thee,
With what grief and unwillingness 'tis forc'd from me?
Yet, in respect I have favour'd thee, I will hear
What thou canst speak to qualify or excuse
Thy readiness to serve this woman's lust,
And wish thou couldst give me such satisfaction
As I might bury the remembrance of it.
Look up, we stand attentive.

Paris   O dread Caesar,
To hope for life, or plead in the defence
Of my ingratitude, were again to wrong you.
I know I have deserv'd death; and my suit is
That you would hasten it; yet, that your highness
When I am dead (as sure I will not live)
May pardon me, I'll only urge my frailty,
Her will, and the temptation of that beauty
Which you could not resist. How could poor I, then,
Fly that which follow'd me, and Caesar sued for?
This is all. And now your sentence.

Caesar   Which I know not
How to pronounce. Oh, that thy fault had been
But such as I might pardon! If thou hadst
In wantonness, like Nero, fir'd proud Rome,

Betray'd an army, butcher'd the whole Senate,
Committed sacrilege, or any crime
The justice of our Roman laws calls death,
I had prevented any intercession
And freely sign'd thy pardon.

Paris   But for this,
Alas, you cannot, nay, you must not, sir;
Nor let it to posterity be recorded
That Caesar, unreveng'd, suffer'd a wrong
Which if a private man should sit down with it,
Cowards would baffle him.

Caesar   With such true feeling
Thou arguest against thyself that it
Works more upon me than if my Minerva
(The grand protectress of my life and empire)
On forfeit of her favour, cried aloud,
'Caesar, show mercy!' and, I know not how,
I am inclin'd to it. Rise. I'll promise nothing;

                                        Paris rises

Yet clear thy cloudy fears, and cherish hopes.
What we must do, we shall do. We remember
A tragedy we oft have seen with pleasure,
Call'd *The False Servant*.

Paris   Such a one we have, sir.

Caesar   In which a great lord takes to his protection
A man forlorn, giving him ample power
To order and dispose of his estate
In his absence, he pretending then a journey.
But yet with this restraint, that on no terms
(This lord suspecting his wife's constancy,
She having play'd false to a former husband)
The servant, though solicited, should consent,
Though she commanded him, to quench her flames.

Paris	That was indeed the argument.
Caesar	And what Didst thou play in it?
Paris	The false servant, sir.
Caesar	Thou didst indeed. Do the players wait without?
Paris	They do, sir, and prepar'd to act the story Your majesty mention'd.
Caesar	Call 'em in. Who presents The injur'd lord?

Enter Aesopus, Latinus, a boy dressed for a lady.

Aesopus	'Tis my part, sir.
Caesar	Thou didst not Do it to the life. We can perform it better. Off with the robe and wreath. Since Nero scorn'd not The public theatre, we in private may Disport ourselves. This cloak and hat, without Wearing a beard, or other property, Will fit the person.
Aesopus	Only, sir, a foil, The point and edge rebutted, when you are To do the murder.[*Offers a foil*] If you please to use this, And lay aside your own sword.
Caesar	By no means. In jest or earnest this parts never from me. We'll have but one short scene. That where the lady In an imperious way commands the servant To be unthankful to his patron. When My cue's to enter, prompt me. Nay, begin, And do it sprightly. Though but a new actor, When I come to execution you shall find No cause to laugh at me.

Latinus	In the name of wonder,
	What's Caesar's purpose?
Aesopus	There is no contending.
Caesar	Why, when?
Paris	I am arm'd,
	And stood Death now within my view, and his
	Unevitable dart aim'd at my breast,
	His cold embraces should not bring an ague
	To any of my faculties, till his pleasures
	Were serv'd and satisfied.
Boy	Must we entreat,
	That were born to command? Or court a servant,
	That owes his food and clothing to our bounty,
	For that which thou ambitiously shouldst kneel for?
	Urge not in thy excuse the favours of
	Thy absent lord, or that thou stand'st engag'd
	For thy life to his charity; nor thy fears
	Of what may follow, it being in my power
	To mould him any way.
Paris	As you may me,
	In what his reputation is not wounded,
	Nor I, his creature, in my thankfulness suffer.
	I know you're young and fair; be virtuous too,
	And loyal to his bed.
Boy	Can my love-sick heart
	Be cur'd with counsel? My desires admit not
	The least delay; and therefore instantly
	Give me to understand what I shall trust to.
	For I am refus'd, and not enjoy
	Those ravishing pleasures from thee I run mad for,
	I'll swear unto my lord at his return
	(Making what I deliver good with tears)
	That brutishly thou wouldst have forc'd from me

	What I make suit for. And then but imagine What 'tis to die, with these words, 'slave' and 'traitor', With burning corrosives writ upon thy forehead, And live prepar'd for't.
Paris	[*Aside*] This he will believe Upon her information, 'tis apparent, And then I am nothing; and of two extremes, Wisdom says choose the less. – Rather than fall Under your indignation, I will yield. This kiss, and this, confirms it.
Aesopus	Now, sir, now.
Caesar	I must take them at it?
Aesopus	Yes, sir, be but perfect.
Caesar	O villain! Thankless villain! – I should talk now; But I have forgot my part. But I can do, Thus, thus, and thus.

Kills Paris

Paris	Oh! I am slain in earnest.
Caesar	'Tis true; and before life leave thee, let the honour I have done thee in thy death bring comfort to thee. To confirm I lov'd thee, 'twas my study To make thy end more glorious, to distinguish My Paris from all others, and in that Have shown my pity. Nor would I let thee fall By a centurion's sword, or have thy limbs Rent piecemeal by the hangman's hook (however Thy crime deserv'd it), but as thou didst live Rome's bravest actor, 'twas my plot that thou Shouldst die in action, and to crown it, die With an applause enduring to all times, By our imperial hand. [*Paris dies*]. His soul is freed From the prison of his flesh; let it mount upward.

And for this trunk, when that the funeral pile
Hath made it ashes, we'll see it enclos'd
In a golden urn; poets adorn his hearse
With their most ravishing sorrows, and the stage
For ever mourn him, and all such as were
His glad spectators weep his sudden death,
The cause forgotten in his epitaph.

Exeunt. A sad music, the Players bearing off Paris' body,
Caesar and the rest following.

Enter Parthenius, Stephanos, Guard

Parthenius   [*To the Guard*]
Keep a strong guard upon him, and admit not
Access to any, to exchange a word
Or syllable with him, till the emperor pleases
To call him to his presence.

Exit Guard

The relation
That you have made me, Stephanos, of this late
Strange passion in Caesar, doth amaze me.
The machine on which all this mischief mov'd,
Domitia, receiv'd again to grace!

Stephanos   Nay, courted to it,
Such is the impotence of his affection.
Yet, to conceal his weakness, he gives out
The people made suit for her, whom they hate more
Than civil war, or famine. But take heed,
My lord, that nor in your consent nor wishes
You lent or furtherance or favour to
The plot contriv'd against her. Should she prove it,
Nay, doubt it only, you are a lost man,
Her power o'er doting Caesar being now
Greater than ever.

Parthenius   'Tis a truth I shake at.
And when there's opportunity –

Stephanos	Say but 'Do', I am yours, and sure.
Parthenius	I will stand one trial more, And then you shall hear from me.
Stephanos	Now observe The fondness of this tyrant, and her pride.

Enter Caesar and Domiita

Caesar	Nay, all's forgotten.
Domitia	It may be on your part.
Caesar	Forgiven too, Domitia; 'tis a favour That you should welcome with more cheerful looks. Can Caesar pardon what you durst not hope for And yet must sue to her whose guilt is Wash'd off by his mercy?
Domitia	I ask'd none; And I should be more wretched to receive Remission for what I hold no crime. I dared thy utmost fury. Though thy flatterers Persuade thee that thy murders, lusts, and rapes Are virtues in thee, and what pleases Caesar (Though never so unjust) is right and lawful, Or work in thee a false belief that thou Art more than mortal, yet I to thy teeth (When circl'd with thy guards, thy rods, thy axes, And all the ensigns of thy boasted power) Will say Domitian, nay, add to it Caesar, Is a weak, feeble man, a bondman to His violent passions, and in that my slave, Nay, more my slave than my affections made me To my lov'd Paris.
Caesar	Can I live, and hear this? Or hear, and not revenge it? Come, you know

The strength that you hold on me; do not use it
With too much cruelty, for though pardon's granted,
Reason may teach me to shake off the yoke
Of my fond dotage.

Domitia   Never; do not hope it;
It cannot be. Thou being my beauty's captive,
And not to be redeem'd, my empire's larger
Than thine, Domitian, which I'll exercise
With rigour on thee, for my Paris' death.
And when I have forc'd those eyes, now red with fury,
To drop down tears, in vain spent to appease me,
I know thy fervour such to my embraces
(Which shall be, though kneel'd for, still denied thee)
That thou with languishment shall wish my actor
Did live again, so thou mightst be his second
To feed upon these delicates, when he's sated.

Caesar   Oh, my Minerva!

Domitia   [*points to a statue of Minerva*]
                          There she is, invoke her:
She cannot arm thee with ability
To draw thy sword on me, my power being greater;
Or only say to thy centurions,
'Dare none of you to do what I shake to think on,
And in this woman's death remove the Furies
That every hour afflict me?' Lamia's wrongs
When thy lust forc'd me from him, are in me
At the height reveng'd; nor would I outlive Paris
But that thy love, increasing with my hate,
May add unto thy torments; so with all
Contempt I can, I leave thee.

                                        Exit Domitia

Caesar   I am lost
Nor am I Caesar. When I first betray'd

The freedom of my faculties and will
To this imperious siren, I laid down
The empire of the world and of myself
At her proud feet. Sleep all my ireful powers?
Wake, my anger!
For shame, break through this lethargy, and appear
With usual terror and enable me
(Since I wear not a sword to pierce her heart,
Nor have a tongue to say this 'Let her die'),
Though 'tis done with a fever-shaken hand,

Pulls out a table-book

To sign her death. Assist me, great Minerva,
And vindicate thy votary! [*Writes*] So; she's now
Among the list of those I have proscrib'd,
And are, to free me of my doubts and fears,
To die tomorrow.

Stephanos   That same fatal book
Was never drawn yet, but some men of rank
Were mark'd out for destruction.

Parthenius   I begin
To doubt myself.

Exit Stephanos

Caesar   Who waits there?

Parthenius   [*Comes forward*]   Caesar.

Caesar   So!
These that command arm'd troops quake at my frowns
And yet a woman slights 'em. Where's the wizard
We charg'd you to fetch in?

Parthenius   Ready to suffer
What death you please t' appoint him.

Caesar   Bring him in.

Exit Parthenius

Enter Ascletario, Tribunes, Guard

We'll question him ourself. – Now you that hold
Intelligence with the stars, and dare prefix
The day and hour in which we are to part
With life and empire, punctually foretelling
The means and manner of our violent end,
As you would purchase credit to your art,
Resolve me, since you are assur'd of us,
What fate attends yourself?

Ascletario   I have had long since
A certain knowledge, and as sure as thou
Shalt die tomorrow, being the fourteenth of
The kalends of October, the hour five,
Spite of prevention, this carcass shall be
Torn and devour'd by dogs – and let that stand
For a firm prediction.

Caesar   Are we the great disposer
Of life and death, yet cannot mock the stars
In such a trifle? Hence with the impostor!
And having cut his throat, erect a pile
Guarded with soldiers till his cursed trunk
Be turn'd to ashes. Upon forfeit of
Your life, and theirs, perform it.

Ascletario   'Tis in vain.
When what I have foretold is made apparent,
Tremble to think what follows.

Caesar   Drag him hence,
And do as I command you.

                    The Tribunes and Guard bear off Ascletario

                              I was never
Fuller of confidence, for having got
The victory of my passions, in my freedom

From proud Domitia (who shall cease to live
Since she disdains to love), I rest unmov'd;
And in defiance of prodigious meteors,
That scrupulous thing styl'd conscience is sear'd up,
And since I have subdu'd triumphant love
I will not deify pale captive fear,
Nor in a thought receive it. For till thou,
Wisest Minerva, that from my first youth
Hast been my sole protectress, dost forsake me,
Not Junius Rusticus' threaten'd apparition,
Nor what this soothsayer but e'en now foretold
(Being things impossible to human reason)
Shall in a dream disturb me. Bring my couch there.

Enter Servants with couch and exeunt

A sudden but a secure drowsiness
Invites me to repose myself. Let music
With some choice ditty second it. I'the meantime,
Rest there, dear book, which open'd when I wake
Shall make some sleep for ever.

Lays the book under his pillow. Music and song. Caesar sleeps.

Enter Parthenius and Domitia

Domitia   Write my name
In his bloody scroll, Parthenius? The fear's idle;
He durst not, could not.

Parthenius   I can assure nothing,
But the bloody catalogue being still about him,
As he sleeps you dare peruse it.

Domitia   I would not be caught
With too much confidence. By your leave, sir.

Takes book

Ha!

No motion! You lie uneasy, sir;
Let me mend your pillow.

Parthenius   Have you it?

Domitia   'Tis here.

Caesar   Oh!

Parthenius   You have wak'd him; softly, gracious madam,
              While we are unknown, and then consult at leisure.

Exeunt Parthenius and Domitia

ichard III : MacBeth

A dreadful music sounding, enter Junius Rusticus and Palphurius Sura,
with bloody swords; they wave them over his head. Caesar in his sleep,
troubled, seems to pray to the image; they scornfully take it away.

Caesar   Whither have
              These Furies borne thee? Let me rise, and follow!
              I am bath'd o'er with the cold sweat of death,
              And am depriv'd of organs to pursue
              These sacrilegious spirits. Am I at once
              Robb'd of my hopes and being? No! I live,

Rises distractedly

              Yes, live, and have discourse to know myself
              Of gods and men forsaken. What accuser
              Within me cries aloud, I have deserv'd it
              In being just to neither? Who dares speak this?
              Am I not Caesar? How! Again repeat it?
              Presumptuous traitor, thou shalt die! What traitor?
              He that hath been a traitor to himself
              And stands convicted here. Yet who can sit
              A competent judge o'er Caesar? Caesar. Yes,
              Caesar by Caesar's sentenc'd, and must suffer.
              Minerva cannot save him. Ha! Where is she?
              Where is my goddess? Vanish'd! I am lost then.
              No, 'twas no dream, but a most real truth,
              That Junius Rusticus and Palphurius Sura,
              Although their ashes were cast in the sea,

Were by their innocence made up again,
As at their deaths they threaten'd. And methought
Minerva ravish'd hence, whisper'd that she
Was for my blasphemies disarm'd by Jove,
And could no more protect me. Yes, 'twas so;

Thunder and lightning

His thunder does confirm it, against which,
Howe'er it spare the laurel, this proud wreath
Is no assurance.

Enter three Tribunes

          Ha! Come you resolv'd
To be my executioners?

First Tribune   Allegiance
And faith forbid that we should life an arm
Against your sacred head.

Second Tribune   We rather sue
For mercy.

Third Tribune   And acknowledge that in justice
Our lives are forfeited for not performing
What Caesar charg'd us.

First Tribune   Nor did we transgress it
In our want of will or care; for being but men
It could not be in us to make resistance,
The gods fighting against us.

Caesar   Speak, in what
Did they express their anger? We will hear it,
But dare not say undaunted.

First Tribune   In brief thus, sir.
The sentence given by your imperial tongue
For the astrologer Ascletario's death
With speed was put in execution.

Caesar	Well.
First Tribune	For his throat cut, his legs bound, and his arms

First Tribune For his throat cut, his legs bound, and his arms
Pinion'd behind his back, the breathless trunk
Was with all scorn dragg'd to the Field of Mars,
And there a pile being rais'd of old dry wood,
Smear'd o'er with oil and brimstone, or what else
Could help to feed or to increase the fire,
The carcass was thrown on it. But no sooner
The stuff that was most apt began to flame,
But suddenly, to the amazement of
The fearless soldier, a sudden flash
Of lightning, breaking through the scatter'd clouds,
With such a horrid violence forc'd its passage,
And as disdaining all heat but itself
In a moment quench'd the artificial fire.
And before we could kindle it again
A clap of thunder follow'd, with such noise
As if then Jove, incens'd against mankind,
Had in his secret purposes determin'd
A universal ruin to the world.
Yet here the wonder ends not, but begins;
For as in vain we labour'd to consume
The witch's body, all the dogs of Rome,
Howling and yelling like to famish'd wolves,
Brake in upon us: and though thousands were
Kill'd in th'attempt, some did ascend the pile
And with their eager fangs seiz'd on the carcass.

Caesar But have they torn it?

First Tribune   Torn it, and devour'd it.

Caesar I then am a dead man, since all predictions
Assure me I am lost. Oh, my lov'd soldiers,
Your emperor must leave you! Yet however
I cannot grant myself a short reprieve,
I freely pardon you. The fatal hour

Steals fast upon me. I must die this morning
By five, my soldiers; that's the latest hour
You e'er must see me living.

First Tribune   Jove avert it!
In our swords lies your fate, and we will guard it.

Caesar   Oh no, it cannot be; it is decreed.
Let proud mortality but look on Caesar,
Compass'd of late with armies, in his eyes
Carrying both life and death, and in his arms
Fathoming the earth; that would be styl'd a god,
Sinking with mine own weight.

First Tribune   Do not forsake
Yourself; we'll never leave you.

Second Tribune   We'll draw up
More cohorts of your guard, if you doubt treason.

Caesar   They cannot save me. The offended gods,
From their envy of my power and greatness here,
Conspire against me.

First Tribune   Endeavour to appease them.

Caesar   'Twill be fruitless;
I am past hope of remission. Yet could I
Decline this dreadful hour of five, these terrors
That drive me to despair would soon fly from me;
And could you but till then assure me –

First Tribune   Yes, sir;
Or we'll fall with you, and make Rome the urn
In which we'll mix our ashes.

Caesar   'Tis said nobly;
I am something comforted. Howe'er, to die
Is the full period of calamity.

                                              Exeunt

SCENE TWO

Enter Parthenius, Domitia, Julia, Caenis, Domitilla,
Stephanos, Sejeius, Entellus

Parthenius	You see we are all condemn'd; there's no evasion. We must do, or suffer.
Stephanos	But it must be sudden. The least delay is mortal.
Domitia	Would I were A man to give it action!
Domitilla	Could I make my approaches, though my stature Does promise little, I have a spirit as daring As hers that can reach higher.
Stephanos	I will take That burden from you, madam. All the art is To draw him from the tribunes that attend him, For could you bring him but within my sword's reach, The world should owe her freedom from a tyrant To Stephanos.
Sejeius	You shall not share alone The glory of a deed that will endure To all posterity.
Entellus	I will put in For a part myself.
Parthenius	Be resolute, and stand close. I have conceiv'd a way, and with the hazard Of my life I'll practise it, to fetch him hither. But then no trifling.
Stephanos	We'll dispatch him, fear not; A dead dog never bites.

Parthenius	Thus then, at all.

Parthenius goes off; the rest stand aside

Enter Caesar and the Tribunes.

Caesar	How slow-pac'd are these minutes! In extremes
	How miserable is the least delay!
	Could I imp feathers to the wings of time,
	Or with as little ease command the sun
	To scourge his coursers up heaven's eastern hill,
	Making the hour I tremble at past recalling,
	My veins and arteries, emptied with fear,
	Would fill and swell again. How do I look?
	Do you yet see Death about me?

First Tribune	Think not of him.
	There is no danger.

Caesar	'Tis well said,
	Exceeding well, brave soldier. Perish all
	Predictions! I grow constant they are false,
	And built upon uncertainties.

First Tribune	This is right.
	Now Caesar's heard like Caesar.

Caesar	We will to
	The camp, and having there confirm'd the soldier
	With a large donative, and increase of pay,
	Some shall – I say no more.

Enter Parthenius

Parthenius	All happiness,
	Security, long life, attend upon
	The monarch of the world!

Caesar	Thy looks are cheerful.

Parthenius	And my relation full of joy and wonder.

Why is the care of your imperial body,
My lord, neglected, the fear'd hour being past,
In which your life was threaten'd?

Caesar   Is't past five?

Parthenius   Past six, upon my knowledge, and in justice
Your clock-master should die, that hath deferr'd
Your peace so long. There is a post new lighted
That brings assur'd intelligence that your legions
In Syria have won a glorious day,
And much enlarg'd your empire. I have kept him
Conceal'd that you might first partake the pleasure
In private, and the Senate from yourself
Be taught to understand how much they owe
To you and to your fortune.

Caesar   Hence, pale fear, then!
Lead me, Parthenius.

First Tribune   Shall we wait you?

Caesar   No.
After losses guards are useful. Know your distance.

                          Exeunt Caesar and Parthenius

Second Tribune How strangely hopes delude men! As I live,
The hour is not yet come.

First Tribune   Howe'er, we are
To pay our duties, and observe the sequel.

                               Exeunt Tribunes

Domitia   I hear him coming. Be constant.

                  Enter Caesar and Parthenius

Caesar   Where, Parthenius,
Is this glad messenger?

Stephanos	Make the door fast. – Here; A messenger of horror.
Caesar	How! Betray'd?
Domitia	No; taken, tyrant!
Caesar	My Domitia In the conspiracy!
Parthenius	Behold this book.
Caesar	Nay, then I am lost. Yet though I am unarm'd I'll fall not poorly.

Overthrows Stephanos

Stephanos	Help me!
Entellus	Thus and thus!
Sejeius	Are you so long a-falling?

They stab Caesar

Caesar	'Tis done, 'tis done basely.

Falls and dies

Parthenius	This is for my father's death.
Domitia	This for my Paris.
Julia	This for thy incest.
Domitilla	This for thy abuse Of Domitilla.

These severally stab him

First Tribune	[*Within*]	Force the doors!

Enter Tribunes

O Mars!
What have you done?

Parthenius	What Rome shall give us thanks for.
Stephanos	Dispatch'd a monster.
First Tribune	Yet he was our prince,

However wicked, and in you 'tis murder,
Which whosoe'er succeeds him will revenge.
[*To Domitia*] Nor will we that serv'd under his command
Consent that such a monster as thyself, the ground
Of all these mischiefs, shall go hence unpunish'd. –
Lay hands on her and drag her to her sentence.
Take up his body. He in death hath paid
For all his cruelties. Here's the difference:
Good kings are mourn'd for after life; but ill,
And such as govern'd only by their will
And not their reason, unlamented fall;
No good man's tear shed at their funeral.

Exeunt

Flourish.

FINIS